the Fire *and*
the Rose

the Fire *and* the Rose

Human Core Needs and Personal Transformation

Robert Griffith Turner, Jr., Ph.D.

HarperCollins*Publishers*

HarperCollins books may be purchased for educational, business, or sales promotional use. For information please write: Special Markets Department, HarperCollins Publishers, Inc., 10 East 53rd Street, New York, NY 10022.

FIRST EDITION

Designed by Maura Fadden Rosenthal

Library of Congress Cataloging-in-Publication Data

Turner, Robert, 1938–
    The fire and the rose : human core needs and personal transformation / Robert G. Turner. — 1st ed.
        p.   cm.
    ISBN 0-06-017330-0
    1. Self-actualization (Psychology)   2. Self-perception.   3. Centering (Psychology) I. Title.
    BF637.S4T836   1996
    158'.1—dc20   95-38489

96 97 98 99 00 ❖/HC 10 9 8 7 6 5 4 3 2 1

For:
Adrienne
Erin
Robin
Allyn
Devin
Brenden

Keep the peace of the Circle and take your love where
it is needed.

And the end of all our exploring
Will be to arrive where we started
And know the place for the first time.
Through the unknown remembered gate
When the last of earth left to discover
Is that which was the beginning; . . .

And all shall be well and
All manner of thing shall be well
When the tongues of flame are in-folded
Into the crowned knot of fire
And the fire and the rose are one.

T. S. Eliot, "Little Gidding"

CONTENTS

CONTENTS

ACKNOWLEDGMENTS

This work evolved from my long, ongoing struggle to make sense of my experience and that of my Terran shipmates. We seem to be on a journey from mystery into mystery. I have never been able to let the mystery alone. I don't suppose I ever will. In any case it is difficult to say precisely who contributed what to the birth of this book. I have taken ideas and insights from so many people.

My editor in Blacksburg, Netta Smith, provided a catalyst composed of enthusiasm, editorial competence, and unflagging belief in the value of my work. I cannot imagine this book having been born without her help. Charles Jervis provided a wealth of commentary and insight into an earlier version of the manuscript, and Kiva Rogers Ryan provided helpful comments and insights that are much appreciated.

My students at Virginia Tech and at Radford University provided feedback and insights which helped form the emerging content and structure of matrix theory. I will always be grateful to them.

Among my professional colleagues at Virginia Tech, Dr. George Hillery has long been my academic mentor. George encouraged me to write this book. He also acted as midwife to many of my ideas—although he is not responsible for my conjecture or my errors, known or unknown. Dr. Peggy DeWolf offered helpful insights and comments on the manuscript with moral support. In ways they may not have been aware of, Dr. Donald Shoemaker and Dr. Brad Hertel provided me support and encouragement when I was not getting much of either. Dr. Karl Pribram offered helpful comments on two chapters of an earlier form of the manuscript for which I am grateful—even though I may not have been able to fully accommodate his suggestions.

At HarperCollins, Larry Ashmead offered me the amazing grace of finding value in my work, while Jason Kaufman has been a friendly, supportive, and helpful guide to the world of books-about-to-be-published.

Linda Hyatt, my agent, made the suggestions that led to the connections, that led to the contract, that published the book that Robert wrote. Linda, of course, means "beautiful" in several languages.

PREFACE

This is a book about finding our way in a world that is heading toward transformation. While it is woven around an intellectual structure intended as the foundation for a new kind of human science, this book is not for specialists. Instead, the ideas in a system of thought called matrix theory are drawn out of their intellectual framework and offered as tools for personal growth. If what is in this book can be summed up in a single sentence, it is this:

You are what you want.

But here is the hook: We are not aware of what we want; much of what we think we want is not what we need; much of what we think we need is not what we want.

We have four elemental, universal needs. They are:

The Need to Give and Receive Love	The Need for Identity and Approval in a Social World
The Need for Cosmic Grounding	The Need to Nurture and Protect the Body

We have these needs, but we are not normally aware of their power, their innocence, or their geometry in the fourfold structure of our consciousness. In particular, we seldom understand our needs for giving and receiving love or for cosmic grounding. As we will explain in the pages ahead, these are the needs that relate *who we are* to *the cosmos that gives us our existence.* They are our fundamental relating needs. In fact, we will simply call them our "relational core needs."

This book is about rediscovering all of our core needs, but especially those that help us experience who we are and our place in the universe. As it turns out, such a journey of discovery can proceed by fairly simple methods. (Not necessarily easy, just simple.) Meanwhile, there is a crucial obstacle to self-discovery that must be addressed before any other needs are considered. It is this: We have been taught to think about ourselves and about the world with "half our consciousness." In particular, we have been taught to ignore or to devalue our direct inner experience. We have been taught (and often convinced) that the real world is made up of material objects that are mainly nonsentient and indifferent to our existence. Atoms, rocks, molecules, oceans, concrete, asphalt. Worse, we have been mostly convinced that the "real knowledge" describing this material world comes in words and word-spun concepts. Where words fail or where concepts do not exist, we imagine a sea of mystery. Creatures brought to our attention from that foamy, dreamlike sea—tales of near-death survivors, of mysterious healings, of telepathy, of reincarnation—are pushed away from the "reality" of our daily lives and largely ignored. We are mostly convinced that what is not reported in the 6:30 news, *Nightline,* or *The New York Times,* can have no genuine reality.

Our sense of what may be real about ourselves and the universe is often so limited that it would be comical if it were not so dangerous. By way of simile, imagine that reality (whatever that may be) could be transmitted to us on a spectrum of signal frequencies ranging, say, from 10 oscillations per second to 10,000. Mostly, you and I are like creatures huddling around a receiver designed to receive a range of 40 to 60 oscillations, nodding sagely to each other about the demonic strangeness of the occasional intrusion of a 65-hertz signal.

The simile probably grossly underestimates the scope of our restless unknowing, but let me translate its import here. In simplest terms, we are largely convinced that there is one way of knowing ourselves and the world—the way of thinking-with-words (or numbers) about things-that-can-be-weighed-and-measured. Period.

To say that this dogged "half-wittedness" is an error is a bit like describing a major hurricane as a rotating breeze. Fortunately, in the secret thoughts and feelings of almost anyone you've ever met or ever will meet, the depth and breadth of our studied ignorance is often sensed if not expressed.

In these pages, the inner knowing we hide from ourselves cannot be revealed. That would be expecting too much. What we will do is provide a way of seeing into the sea of mystery we call our "self." We will do that by unfolding a new kind of map for guiding our insight. Through that insight, we will open a door into the other way of knowing that must balance the way of words and thinking.

To understand our needs—our core needs—is to move toward self-awareness. However, to move toward self-awareness requires us to understand that we have two ways of knowing, not one. We will call these two ways the *relational* and the *objective*.

Relational knowing is the matrix of all knowing. It is direct, wordless. It draws on our feeling and on our intuition, for these are the qualities of the self that link us to our Source. Relational knowing is what allows us to explore the inner world, which is our connection to each other and to the cosmos. It is our passport to what we want and, therefore, to who we are.

Objective knowing, on the other hand, is linear, rational, and, always, knowing at second hand. It is dependent on words, symbols, and ordinary thinking. Objective knowing is necessary for living in a body in time. But it is ultimately deceptive and poisonous if it is not mediated and informed by the deeper knowing of feeling and intuition.

Among other things, relational knowing allows us to become aware that most of what we imagine about ourselves comes from the social world into which we are born. These imaginings, arranged around the beliefs and attitudes we have been taught, are what we will call the ego. All egos have one thing in common. They are structures of attack and defense we develop to survive in a human social world. They are defensive and hostile because social worlds do not allow us to understand our core needs or form effective strategies to meet them. Some cultures may have done better than others in grasping our core needs, but there are none I know of that are (or were) "egoless." The more out of balance a culture is through emphasizing certain core needs and devaluing others, the more defensive and intractable is the typical ego that develops in it. Modern Western social worlds are seriously out of balance.

You may think of this book as a guide to discovering what you want. Included in the guide is a compass, called the Brenden Matrix, which may be used for restoring a balanced experience of our core needs and for choosing. What may be chosen (for there is nothing else, finally, worth choosing) is the direct understanding that, beyond your ego, there is a self that is safe and at home in the universe.

1

A Door Opening

What fortitude the soul contains,
That it can so endure
The accent of a coming foot,
The opening of a door!

Emily Dickinson

EARTH TREMORS

We are alive together in the midst of an era of escalating planetary change. The change is about more than population growth,
burning rain forests, Wal-Martized communities, where all the
jobs are owned by someone you've never met and never will. It is
about more than overflowing prisons, diets for every anxious
occasion, or any of the other banalities and insanities recorded
for us daily in the newspapers and on *A Current Affair*. You and
I, our social worlds, and the planet itself are undergoing a transformation. What was yesterday has no words for tomorrow, no
language.

In terms of scientific models, what is happening is something called "whole-system change." But that expression is, somehow, too clinical, too neatly trimmed of the tendrils of its implications. It does not recognize the mystery beyond the convergence of ecological, social, and consciousness changes weaving themselves together on the time loom we call reality. It does not, perhaps because it cannot, capture the high strangeness that is stirring quantum physics and alternative communities, near-death experiences, and the weird uncertainties of UFO "abductee" accounts, chaos theory, and vanishing stratospheric ozone in a single bubbling caldron of transmutation. It is, perhaps, closer to the truth to say that our Earth and all its life, which is a caterpillar, will become, out of a cocoon spun of chaos, a butterfly with no name.

You and I are part of that which is changing. The mother Earth, the willow and the hurricane, shopping malls and thrift accounts, the lazy weight of breakers on a Carolina shore, digital cascades of options over fiber-optic cables, thoughtfulness and desire, moonlight images of gravestones and wedding rings, seekers in meditation, children at play—we are all of that. We are the caterpillar at the edge of transformation.

As we come to understand this, we realize that each of us has only two choices, moment by moment. We may drift in the sticky, familiar currents of denial, or we may attempt to discover our place in what is happening. We can choose to do that. That is why we are here; that is why I am writing these words and, quite possibly, why you are reading them.

Of course, you may not believe any of this. The sky is not falling and Chicken Little just needs a little Valium. Perhaps. As it turns out, a conviction that the Earth system, with its impudent, innocent, violent burden of humankind, is undergoing transformation is not a prerequisite for whatever use you may make of this book. It is only necessary and fair that you should know the timbre of urgency behind what is written here. It is my conviction, shared by many others, that our current era is one of unprecedented change.[1] Certainly that change will encompass endings. Humankind's violent alteration of Earth's biosphere is changing our species' relationship to the web of life. At the same time, the challenges of our planetary crisis may signal breathtaking leaps into vibrant futures, into unexpected beginnings. The balance between anguish and freedom will lie in the nature of our choices.

This book is about how we may make these choices.

A Tool Kit for Making Sense of This Book

While you need not subscribe to the notion that our world is heading toward an ending and a beginning, it is needful that you be willing to consider three dimensions of one idea if you are to find use for what is written here:

1. Human life is full of paradox.

2. Making sense of paradox requires a different way of thinking, the way understood in science by a concept called "complementarity." In practical, human terms, it is a way of thinking that allows us to find the place of resolution between the knowing of the heart and the planning of the head.

3. Our social worlds carefully teach us how not to think that way.

Paradox

Human experience is laced together and saturated in paradox. For every yes there is a no, for every no a yes, and often they seem to be utterly contradictory. Paradox seems sometimes to tear us apart, to render life and human choice all but untenable. Still, the effort to avoid paradox is the equivalent of sleepwalking.

We both *have* a body and seem to *be* a body. We must embrace life in the face of the visages of death. The real world seems only a visible, sensory landscape flowing along in terms of immutable laws—gravity, entropy, momentum—when everything truly important to us is invisible. Love, meaning, joy, the human soul are without discernible mass or velocity.

In Western culture, paradox blooms in every institution, in every field of inquiry or endeavor. We have dreamed together an economic system in which we are assured that the pursuit of individual greed will produce the greatest good for the greatest number. We have clothed individualism in an armor of competition, assuring that our victories require the defeat of those whose applause might affirm our achievements. We are asked again and again to choose between living and making a living. Out of the peculiar twists and turns of the Western ideas of romantic love, we have replaced the grail quest with the quest for the "one and only." Genital sexuality and domestic commitment strangle each other like the two serpents of the caduceus. We crave love and would possess a beloved. Yet every act of possessing blocks love's channels.

These paradoxes are not arcane, not hidden—we all live with them. Popular songs tell us all about it. "Take this job and shove it" is a lyric to alienation for those who have never read Marx. "Love only blooms when it's on the vine; handful of thorns and you know you've missed it," goes the song. "Lose your love when you say the word 'mine.'"

In our philosophical presumptions, we are asked to live on a bridge between mind and matter, between subjectivity and objectivity, never knowing quite where the bridge is. When we would seek the essence of things, we must bear Kant's inheritance—even if we know nothing of his philosophy. For his irreconcilable gap between phenomena we may experience and their essence (noumena) is now built into our consciousness. Kant's synthetic a prioris and Aristotle's logic, Newton's apple and Descartes's chasm between mind and matter, are parts and pieces of our cultural DNA. They are "cultigens" that order our lives as surely as the peptide bar-coding sequences that make your eyes blue and mine brown.

Efforts to plumb the depths of meaning on a spiritual quest lead us down narrow paths hedged about with apparent irreconcilables. "The first shall be last" in a world where nice guys finish last. "Love your enemies" when we do not know how to love our children. When we would judge and rank everything, the great spiritual traditions ask us to surrender judgment. When we would condemn, clothed in righteous pain and fury, we are asked to forgive. When we would attack, feeling compelled to defend ourselves, struggling for our due, we are told to offer the other cheek, the open hand. Harmlessness.

COMPLEMENTARITY

If paradox is ever resolved for us, it is by grasping and entering into a truce with a peculiar property in reality called complementarity. Although that term originates in quantum physics (from Niels Bohr), it is, in fact, an ancient idea and not just about physics at all. It is about the nature of paradox and how to deal with it. It is about balancing the knowing of insight and intuition with our drive to manipulate and control the world through thinking.

Another physicist, Erwin Schroedinger, once commented that the opposite of a profound truth is often another profound truth. We live in bodies in time, for example. We live, yet we die. (There are the "yes" and the "no.") And what is the paradoxical opposite of this profound truth? What reality encompasses both living and dying? It is this: We are light-energy-mind creatures that do not require bodies. We exist before and after a tour of the space-time domain. At the deepest level of human understanding, that is the sort of thing complementarity is about. For every contradictory "yes-no" in our experience, there is a "something" that transcends and resolves the contradiction. Would you change something in your life? Would you like to lose weight, for example? The rule of paradox teaches us that the very effort to do so will make the problem more intense and bothersome. "Thinking" a life condition (worrying about it, talking to ourselves about it, making images and scenarios in our mind about it) makes the condition more and more a "problem." Sometimes, of course, there is no actual physiological problem at all. Especially for women in our society, "overweight" may simply be the weight appropriate to one's body type and metabolism. But, assuming one is not at a healthy or appropriate weight level, let us say the idea "I will lose weight" is the "yes" you would prefer. Fine. This "yes" will, inevitably, be countered by a "no"—the stunning resistance we encounter when we try to solve a "problem."

So how do you lose weight by the rule of paradox? By an inner decision called "intent" (which will be explained further as we go along). The heart of intent is in accepting a paradoxical idea: *There is no problem; I have everything I need.* The change that is intended proceeds, then, in a balance of action, best guided by intuition. The "yes" part of the action may involve forming exercise and diet habits that are, eventually, pleasant to live with. The resistance or "no" part of the matter is dealt with by releasing judgment of what you are doing (by simply doing and not by thinking). Your intent is to alter your body weight. Having formed the intent (and every time it comes to mind after that), you release it. You let it go with an attitude of simple acceptance and, as someone has put it, you "allow the universe to handle the details." Intent is incredibly powerful; it is what underlies our existence. Every condition and situation in your life right this moment is related to your patterns of intent, conscious or unconscious. When your power of intent is clear and conscious, it resolves paradox. And, if what you intend is in alignment with what you truly want and who you truly are, it will happen. Period.

To be sure, grasping paradox and discovering the power of intent, of our wordless, inner decisions, is difficult. These principles go against everything we have been taught. But then, self-knowledge is difficult too—and without some grasp of paradox, self-knowledge is more or less impossible.

Complementarity is real, by the way, it is not just an esoteric idea. In the physical world it is represented by oddities like the nature of light. Observed one way, light appears as waves, rather like the ripples in a pond. Viewed in a different way, it acts like particles with specific measurable mass and location we call photons. What the principle of complementarity tells us is that light is not waves or particles, not A or B, but both. The difference between A and B is not in light, but in our way of observing it. In human experience, complementarity is present in its most embracing form in this fact: We humans have two ways of knowing. We may call these the *relational* and the *objective*.

The example of losing weight by the principle of paradox gives us an illustration of both ways of knowing. Intent draws on direct, clear intuition and feeling. It is an inner decision (not a thought babble in your mind). You may intend to relate to the world in a different way, to change your relational mode (way of being-in-relationship). The actions evolving from that intent— exercise, diet changes—require objective, practical knowledge, like where to get fresh fish or how to use a Nordic Track.

Relational knowing is direct and does not require us to name it—although we will not fail to try. It is the knowing of feeling, of the heart, of intuition, which is the glimmering in us of things glimpsed through a glass darkly. Relational knowing is the matrix of what may be in the next moment, of potential, of meaning, and of the vitality of existing. The languages of poetry, art, dance, drama—and love in all its forms—are relational languages. Above all, it should be remembered that it is through intuition and feeling, through directly seeing how we are "in-relationship," that we may transcend paradox.

Objective knowing is the way of thought and rationality. It is also the domain of paradox, the place where, for every "yes" there is a "no." We honor and celebrate objective knowing in Western culture, from its fluorescence in Athens to the European Renaissance to the rise of modern science. In pursuit of a freedom we sense we have lost, we honor our objectlike separateness in the Western credos of individualism and human rights. Yet objective knowing is limited. It is clothed always in words and symbols; it is formed in the grammars of spoken languages, in the protocols of logic or rhetoric that would straighten the hems of these symbol garments. Objective knowing is knowing at second hand. A plan for a cathedral is not the cathedral; a model of the circulatory system is not a living capillary or a throbbing aorta. The word "hate" is not the sterile void of human fury.

Relational and objective knowing are like the waves and particles of light. Michael Polanyi, attempting to name this complementarity, put it in these simple words: "We always know more than we can say."[2] Human consciousness is not relational or objective—it is both. Human experience is not sublime poetic insight or the touch of lovers' hands; it is not sink traps that keep the air circulating in our plumbing systems or tables of organization for an infantry battalion. It is both of these kinds of things in balance or in chaos, in order or in reordering. We live in time and out of time, in being and in becoming, in a body and beyond bodies, in dreams and in balance sheets.

We must understand this. We are heart and head, soul and body. We are both in relationship and observers of things that are related. Finding the balance of the relational and the objective in our experience, moment by moment, is the essence of choosing.

The meeting of the two modes of knowing is the junction where meaning is born.

We must also understand that there are powerful forces around us and within us that deny all of this. They are the forces of the social worlds we live in, spun of the preconceptions built into language, hemmed about with beliefs and values that we have made up to imagine we understand who we are and what the world is. Paradox and complementarity mostly get ignored or explained away in the consensus we invent to make a social world. Having made this thing together, this consensus reality, we imagine we must cling to it, white-knuckled and desperate. Our brittle egos and frightened conflicts with each other become life rafts in a sea of dreaming.

To recognize the burning core of paradox at the center of human experience is a necessary disillusion. For beyond our illusions of cosmic mastery, beyond the entranced confusion of our social worlds, the rediscovery of paradox is a door opening.

Beyond the door is mystery; within the mystery is our identity; within our identity we are at home and free.

What This Book Is About

This book offers a map through our time of chaos and reordering. The map is called "matrix theory." In practical terms, the theory is a guide to some of the important forces that shape our lives, and therefore, it is a guide to understanding and to wiser choices. For the human sciences the ideas in these pages constitute spadework for a new paradigm, an alternative set of assumptions and perceptions about human nature and human social worlds and how these work. For the person trying to make sense of life on Earth at the end of the twentieth century, many of the key ideas of matrix theory are for using.

Perhaps because our human predicament is complex, what we

will explore in these pages has complex implications. But it is not far off the mark to think of matrix theory in terms of a pretty simple idea. What we humans do all day long—human action moment by moment—has the patterns and forms it does because all of us have a matrix, a built-in framework, of four fundamental core needs. These are:

1. The need to give and receive love.
2. The need for identity and approval in a social world.
3. The need to nurture and protect the body.
4. The need for cosmic grounding.

The Need to Give and Receive Love

Most of us know, if we are not numb from the scarring of modern life and its discouragements, that love is what gives our life substance and meaning. Infants that are not held, touched, and loved will languish, even die—no matter if all their immediate bodily needs are attended to. Life without intimate relationships—relationships that allow people to see and hear and touch each other with awareness and concern—is hollow, lonely, and meaningless. The need for love is one of giving and receiving, yet these are in fact same thing. To give love is to have it; to have love is to give it. If that strikes you as cryptic, be assured that the topic of love and its nature will receive more attention before this book is through.

The Need for Identity and Approval in a Social World

The need for identity and acceptance in a social world is profound. Children deprived of security and identity in their social world—as most of us are to some extent—may be crippled as adults. Men who are forced to retire from their jobs—especially if they see their work as the essence of their social identity—frequently die within a year or so. Socrates, accused of corrupting the youth of Athens, chose to take the lethal hemlock rather than accept the option of banishment. Undoubtedly there would have been other city-states that would have given him a home. But Socrates's social world, his identity, was intermingled with Athens, not Syracuse or Corinth.

The Need to Nurture and Protect the Body

The need to nurture and care for our bodies is apparent enough to most of us. We spend an enormous amount of time and energy feeding ourselves, putting on and taking off clothing, worrying about bills, striving to make money. But it is helpful to remember that the essence of meeting our body needs is some level or degree of symbiosis with the Earth system. To meet our body needs, we must be an "ecological self." To take our needed measure of air, water, bread, and shelter from the nurturant potential of the natural environment, we must be a part of the give and take of the Earth system.

The Need for Cosmic Grounding

The cosmic-grounding need may seem the most mysterious of the four needs, mainly because Western social worlds have devalued the spiritual dimension of human experience. Indeed, the very word "spiritual" is often uttered apologetically. It denotes things suspiciously beyond the boundary of reason, lurking too near superstition and far from ordinary experience. The word, for most of us, designates something vague, indescribable, indefinable.

The cosmic-grounding need also tends to get concealed because, more or less unconsciously, we make up substitutes for it—like finding that one special person to love us, achieving success, or even living in a neighborhood we feel reflects our sense of social worth and self-esteem. The cosmic-grounding need, however, is only fulfilled in direct knowing, in concrete personal experience of one's deep identity. In the meantime, we may think of our need for cosmic grounding as the need to feel, to sense, finally to know that the universe has a place for us, for who we are, beyond our social roles or even our bodies.

We have these core needs; they are a part of all of us. The problem is, when we are operating out of our ordinary consciousness, we are usually not connected to them. Or, more precisely, our connections to our core needs are conflicted and out of balance. Because that is the case, we do things all day long that defeat our efforts to get what we need. Matrix theory, going beyond the mere identification of a core in us of elemental needs, attempts to understand why we emphasize some of our needs at the expense of the others and what effects this has.

Therefore, given the idea, the hypothesis, that we humans have four fundamental and universal core needs, the next step is understanding why there are precisely four such needs, and then how the needs are related to each other. That turns out to be a tall order. It is what the rest of this book is about.

In any case, the purpose of our exploration is not trivial. As we begin to become aware of our core needs and the crucial art of knowing their weight and balance, we proceed toward self-awareness, toward what Carl Jung named "individuation." That's what makes matrix theory practical for people who are not anthropologists, sociologists, or psychologists. It provides one kind of guide to life choices that lead to growth and fulfillment.

The term "matrix theory" sounds abstract, like something for physicists or mathematicians, but it is not really about abstract theory. The basic method that has led me to the ideas in this book is, simply, paying attention, tenaciously, year after year, to both my inner and my outer experience. I am attempting to go beyond preconceptions to new ways of seeing and understanding. The value of what I have found, I believe, is its potential for making sense of our shared human experience, for re-discovering the illuminated boundary beyond our dance with pain and confusion.

Here is a main thesis of this book: *As you and I begin to understand that we are part of the currents of growth and change around us as well as within us, we may proceed to a different level of awareness.* At that level of awareness, we may make choices. At that level of awareness we rediscover the power of intent. Below that level of awareness, our choices will be illusions of choice. To imagine, in John Donne's imagery, that you are an "island, entire of itself," is a toxic illusion. When we imagine we are choosing out of this level of awareness, we are, in fact, not choosing at all. We are drifting along in a waking trance, dreaming of choosing.

INTERMEZZO

Among mysteries, I think,
the deepest is One,
the most perplexing, two.
The awakener is three,
while the mystery of four is
the story of the cross we bear.

This next chapter is a guide to some of what we may understand of the mystery of four. It is a first step toward understanding the geometry of our desire nature and its innocence. It is full of intellectual concepts because the fourfold geometry we will consider is also the ground plan of an alternative paradigm for the human sciences.

That need not alarm you. We are all scientists of the experience of being human. Besides, even with all of its implications, citations, premises, epistemological heresies, ontological outrages, hypotheses, and research proposals fully extended, the creature called "matrix theory" collapses again into a manageable form, one you can take into your hands and use as a tool for understanding and for growth.

That is what we intend here. That is what we will do with matrix theory. Only that.

2

Basic Ideas from Matrix Theory

Now I a fourfold vision see,
And a fourfold vision is given to me,
'Tis fourfold in my supreme delight
And threefold in soft Beulah's night
And twofold Always. May God us keep
From Single vision & Newton's sleep!

William Blake, 1802

Matrix theory is an effort to draw together the two ways by which we humans can know, the way of the head and of the heart, of the left brain and the right brain, of the objective mode and the relational mode. It strives toward clearer vision. But to grasp human behavior and social worlds in the stereoscopic vision of balanced knowing requires a different way of thinking. We will not abandon reason or logic, neither will we abandon the knowing of intuition and feeling. Instead, we will try to see things whole by tending to both the right and the left, to the part and to the whole, to that in us which observes and measures and to that in us which enters into relationship.

Before tuning in to the cascade of doubts and questions that are characteristic of any of us when we encounter new ideas, allow yourself to float through this chapter. Use your intuition; let your mind be playful. Play with the ideas. As you go through the rest of the book, you may want to come back to this chapter, to look it over with your critical mind as well as with your intuition. In this way, drawing on both ways of knowing, the ideas and their uses should become sharper and more relevant to you.

Forging the patterns of human behavior and of social worlds are a set of four core needs, the four we introduced in the first chapter. But now imagine that these four basic needs can be better understood in terms of a geometry:

FIGURE 1: THE FOUR CORE NEEDS

The Need to Give and Receive Love	The Need for Identity and Approval in a Social World
The Need for Cosmic Grounding	The Need to Nurture and Protect the Body

Geometry is generally about relationships in space. A right triangle, for example, has particular rules that describe the relationship in the spaces made by our consciousness. But, just as the geometry of a right triangle is about the relationships between points in space, the geometry of the core needs is about particular kinds of relationships between needs. Notice, for example, that the needs on the left are mostly about our inner self, the ones on the right more about the world in which the self dwells. This is a part of what is meant when we speak of the geometry of the core needs.

Here is another fourfold model of human nature and of human experiencing.

FIGURE 2

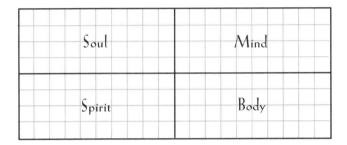

Compare the fourfold matrix of body, mind, soul, and spirit with the arrangement of the core needs. If you can sense a rough fit between the two typologies, you are already catching on to one of the basic ideas behind matrix theory. The idea is this: Fourfold models of human nature and human experience reflect something basic in the nature of consciousness itself.

Of course, the arrangement of the core needs in a fourfold space is intended as a representation, a model that is also a sort of map. It is useful in somewhat the same way that an ideal right triangle is useful. Understanding the triangle's geometry can help us estimate distances from partial information (by use of the Pythagorean theorem). Understanding the geometry of the core needs can help us make estimates about the way social worlds are arranged and how we may make choices that fulfill us. We will see how that geometry works as this book unfolds.

If a fourfold geometry of our core needs is basic to the nature of how consciousness constructs the world, there must be other fourfold typologies of human nature and of human experience. There are. They are quite common, and some are ancient.

FOURFOLD VISIONS, ANCIENT AND MODERN

Many Native American peoples describe four sacred directions, often associated with particular colors. For the Hopi, the four directions are associated with four colors of the corn, which is their traditional sustenance. White, red, yellow, and blue corn are associated with the sacred directions and with special properties of the world. Hopi mythology also speaks of four worlds through which humankind has evolved, this being the fourth.[1]

In kabbalistic tradition, representing the esoteric and mystical knowledge of Judaism, the tetragrammaton *YHVH*, from which we get the word *Jehovah*, stands both for the nameless name of God and for the four worlds.[2]

Through ancient China and much of the rest of the East, an ancient classification of nature was fourfold.[3] An azure dragon was the east, a red bird symbolized the south, a white tiger the west, and a black tortoise the north. This fourfold division was further elaborated in interesting ways, of course, into eight powers, for example, and into an ancient treatise on practical philosophy called the *I Ching*. But the elemental division of the Tao, of the essence of Being-in-process, was seen as being fourfold.

In Plato's *Timaeus* there is a discussion of four elemental properties of the cosmos—earth, air, fire, and water—reflecting an even more ancient fourfold model of nature. These elements would take on elaborated meanings with the medieval alchemists, and there is some convergence between the alchemical elements and the traditional fourfold model of human nature that is shown in Figure 3.

The alchemical notion of four elements was influential in Western thought for a long time. Galen's idea of humans' having four humors or vital substances (yellow bile, green bile, blood, and black bile) was a spin-off from the fourfold model of essential elements in the cosmos, which persisted through the European Middle Ages.

FIGURE 3: THE ALCHEMICAL ELEMENTS AND THE TRADITIONAL TYPOLOGY OF HUMAN NATURE

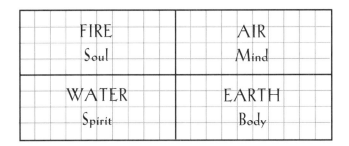

FIRE	AIR
Soul	Mind
WATER	EARTH
Spirit	Body

While many of these ancient fourfold divisions of the cosmos might be dismissed as a peculiar convergence of patterns of prescientific thinking, the matter, I believe, is more subtle than that. And more important.

Among poets, sages, and thinkers who live closer to our times, the appearance of fourfold typologies becomes more interesting and, with respect to the nature of human consciousness, more explicit.

E. F. SCHUMACHER

E. F. Schumacher, author of the seminal work *Small Is Beautiful,* proposed four fields of human knowledge in another work, *A Guide for the Perplexed.*[4] They correspond well not only with the model of four human core needs, but also with four corresponding *existential realms*, which are another face of our deepest long-ings, our deepest nature.

Before I encountered Schumacher's four fields of knowledge, I had imagined a fourfold geometry of what I called existential domains, realms of experience. I called these by the names you see in Figure 4—psyche, ethos, cosmos, and chronos.

FIGURE 4: FOUR DOMAINS OF HUMAN EXPERIENCE

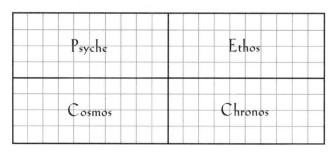

Psyche is the realm of the inner self, of one's heart experienc-ing. It is the domain of the I-am, which is more than a name or even a body. Later on, I would come to associate this domain with what I call the natural self—a notion we will explore later.

Ethos, from the same root that gives us the term "ethics," I asso-ciate with the social world and with questions of appropriate action.

Cosmos is the domain of the transcendent, of consciousness that is Other to my own. It is also concerned with how I may encounter consciousness beyond my own, through intimacy, through empathy, through direct knowing.

Chronos, from the same root that gives us "chronological" and "chronometer," is a Greek word for time. It is our existential domain of time and change, that is, of the sensory world. It is also the realm of adapting to Earth's habitats and of bodily survival.

Schumacher's first field of knowledge, self-knowledge—awareness of the inner self—corresponds with the existential domain of the natural self, psyche. His second field of knowledge, knowledge of others' consciousness, corresponds with the cosmos domain, although he is more interested in encountering the consciousness of other people while I was more concerned with the context or matrix of personal consciousness. His third field of knowledge, regarding, as he puts it, knowing ourselves as others know us in our sociable nature, corresponds with the idea of an ethos domain. Finally, his fourth field of knowledge of the sensory realm is, essentially, the chronos domain.

In Figure 5, we see the core needs (in a shorthand notation); the traditional body, mind, soul, spirit typology; Schumacher's four fields of knowledge; and my existential domains, in a single matrix.

When we put these models of human nature and experience into the same arrangement in space, we are suggesting that, at some basic level, they have the same psychic geometry. And, of course, I believe that is the case.

FIGURE 5: THE CORE NEEDS, A TRADITIONAL DIVISION OF HUMAN EXPERIENCE, SCHUMACHER'S FOUR FIELDS OF KNOWLEDGE, AND FOUR EXISTENTIAL DOMAINS

Love Needs	Social Identity
SOUL	MIND
First Field	Third Field
PSYCHE	ETHOS
Cosmic Grounding	Body Needs
SPIRIT	BODY
Second Field	Fourth Field
COSMOS	CHRONOS

There are three modern thinkers whose ideas contribute more directly and importantly than Schumacher to matrix theory.

William Irwin Thompson, a marvelously eclectic, maverick intel-lectual[5]; Alan Page Fiske, an anthropologist whose discovery of four elementary forms of human social relations offers substantial cross-cultural evidence of an ontogenic (built-in) quality to the fourfold structure of human consciousness; and Carl Jung.[6]

Fiske's work is critical to whatever scientific potential matrix theory may have, while Thompson's work nudges us toward inquiries into the depth and breadth of the apparent fourfold structuring of human experience. Jung's work, more than any other's, provides the psychological base for the core-needs hypothesis. Since this book is aimed at the practical utility of the core-needs model, the work of these three thinkers is only drawn on in the immediate context of our discussions. The extent and significance of their ideas with respect to matrix theory may appear in work aimed at specialists in the human sciences.

THE BRENDEN MATRIX

Carl Jung, the founder of analytical psychology, proposed that we humans have precisely four psychic functions. These are sensa-tion, feeling, thinking, and intuition.[7] As it turns out, this typol-ogy is very useful for making sense of our core needs and how they are related to each other.

FIGURE 6: CARL JUNG'S FOUR PSYCHIC FUNCTIONS IN RELATIONSHIP TO THE CORE NEEDS

Feeling	Thinking
Love Needs	Social Identity
Intuition	Sensation
Cosmic Grounding	Body Needs

For Jung, there is also a fourfold endopsychic realm and, beyond (or deeper), a collective unconscious, ordered as much as it may be by the nature and structure of archetypes. Archetypes may be thought of as shared patterns or themes underlying our awareness of ourselves, each other, the sensory realm, and the realm of the transcendent. The four functions mentioned above he calls *ectopsychic functions,* and they are particular to personal consciousness. But for our purposes, they are an adequate threshold to the recognition of a pattern—that is, the psychic functions and the four core needs are faces of a common source or structure in our essential psychic nature. For each psychic function there is a core need.

Further, the psychic functions are integral. Like the core needs, they are all necessary to our consciousness, to our individuation, to our fulfillment. What Jung said in this regard may be helpful here. In a discussion of his Tavistock Lectures on Analytical Psychology, he said:

> *There are many people who believe that world problems are settled by thinking. But no truth can be established without all four functions. When you have thought the world you have done one-fourth of it; the remaining three-fourths may be against you.*[8]

In discussing these ideas, I find that the association of the thinking function with the social-identity core need is puzzling for some people. Quite simply, the association has to do with the fact that thinking, generally, is about arriving at consensus, or at least about trying to get other people to agree with us. The medium of thinking is language, and language is the glue that orders social worlds. Social identity is about finding our place in these symbol-spun worlds. That is the crux of the matter. The thinking function and social identity are dovetailed. Thinking proceeds in the medium of language and symbol in a dialogue of social-reality construction.

Of course, thinking—as Jung taught us—when not informed from time to time with humbling shocks from the other functions, cannot know much about what may be real and true. What we do know by thinking alone is, essentially, what we decide we may know. For, without quite knowing what we are doing, we enter into a consensus about what meanings we will assign to the words and terms we use. The terms of that consensus are like secondhand garments on a glorious form we feel comfortable keeping well clothed with norms and conventions and customs that have comfortably familiar names. For the medium of thinking is language, and language is about naming. Words are lovely things to play with, but their fascination may fool us into imagining that what we name is what is there. All thought models are scaffolding; all systems of belief are frameworks or guides—useful or misleading. Thinking can make maps. But as a thinker by the name of Korzybski has warned us, the map is not the territory.[9]

Elements of the Brenden Matrix

The convergence of the psychic functions and the core needs with models or typologies like Schumacher's fields of knowledge in the same geometry suggests not only that fourfold structuring is somehow basic in human consciousness, but also that there is a general form behind all of these fourfold typologies. It is this general form, called the Brenden Matrix, that is a fundamental tool we may use for exploring patterns of human behavior, making sense of social worlds, and taking a few steps toward self-knowledge.

The Brenden Matrix, named after a fifth-century Celtic monk who is a patron saint for voyagers—geographical or conceptual—allows us to conceive of a great variety of useful fourfold typologies, all of which may be nested in the same basic geometry, all of which have the same grammar of interrelationship. How that grammar appears to operate, how, for example, our feeling needs are a complement to our body state, or why a social status like our job may get confused with our cosmic-grounding need, will be explored as we proceed.

The general form of the Brenden Matrix is derived from considering the relationship of two complementarities inherent in human experience and human knowing. These are the two modes of knowing—the *relational* and the *objective*—and a *primary existential division*, recognized by William James, between the self and the not-self.[10] It might help to consider these crucial dualities right now as an open matrix. You might want to take a moment to think about various categories you can imagine fitting the four cells.

FIGURE 7: TWO COMPLEMENTARITIES: RELATIONAL AND OBJECTIVE KNOWING AND THE DIVISION OF OUR EXPERIENCE INTO SELF AND NOT-SELF

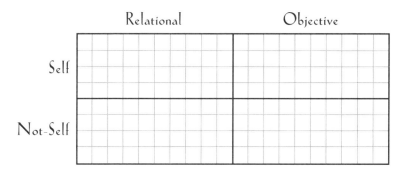

THE RELATIONAL AND THE OBJECTIVE

While the relational and objective modes of knowing are, in fact, part of every moment of ordinary experience, they are not reducible into each other. Relational knowing, the knowing of the poet, the lover, the mother, and the mystic, is not faulty knowing requiring explanations out of logic and rational science; it is valid or invalid in its own terms, in relational terms.

Just as there is objective logic, so there is relational validity. The actual cosmos dwells in both modes; therefore, we cannot comprehend ourselves or the world simply out of the objective mode, out of thought, sensory observation, rationality, or conventional science.

Following the example of Robert Ornstein, one of the pioneers in human-consciousness research, Table 1 gives us some associations often made with the two modes of knowing, adapted for our purposes.[11]

TABLE 1: ASSOCIATIONS WITH THE MODES OF KNOWING[12]

RELATIONAL	OBJECTIVE	SOURCE
Psychological Level		
Right brain	Left brain	Neurophysiology
Feminine	Masculine	Myth, tradition
Tacit knowing	Explicit knowing	Michael Polanyi
Heart	Head	Tradition
Left hand	Right hand	Tradition
Sociocultural Level		
(Social Form or Cultural Mentality)		
Alineal coding	Lineal coding	Dorothy Lee*
Gemeinschaft	Gesellschaft	F. Toennies
Mechanical solidarity	Organic solidarity	Emile Durkheim
Ideational	Sensate	P. A. Sorokin
Myth, Philosophy, Science		
Yin	Yang	Taoism
Receptive	Active	I Ching (China)
Implicate order	Explicate order	David Bohm
Earth	Heaven (sky)	Myth, tradition
I-Thou	I-It	Martin Buber

* Lee, an anthropologist, is looking at types of languages in different types of cultures.

The point of the table is to suggest that there is a long and honorable distinction, made in various ways, between two modes of knowing or of expression. This distinction is often represented as a fundamental duality of complementary principles in the cosmos itself. In short, the two ways of knowing are built into our consciousness.

THE PRIMARY EXISTENTIAL DIVISION

We divide the world always into domains of the self and of the not-self. The American psychologist and philosopher William James actually used the expressions "me" and "not-me" to discuss this observation in his writings on human psychology.[13] The idea is the same, and it is pretty obvious (even if its implications are not). We divide up everything we are aware of into two categories: "me"—which is part of my self—or "not-me"—which is not part of my self. Your feeling of pleasure when you eat chocolate is "me." Your nose is "me." A dogwood tree is "not-me." The badness of Adolf Hitler is "not-me." And so on.

But here is an example to help you see that what is "obvious" in this division of daily experience is, in fact, not all that obvious. Think of spinach. Better yet, get ready to eat some spinach. Notice that you will have a consciousness of spinach that includes word associations (Popeye, maybe), odor associations (vinegar if you're from the South), and feelings (pleasant or unpleasant), among other things. Now, having eaten your spinach (doing what some internal parent commands), consider the adventure of having eaten spinach. Notice, if you will, that there is no clear boundary between you and your spinach. For one thing, it exists for you because it is in your awareness, in your consciousness. Further, now that you've eaten it, "your" enzymes are breaking it up for transport to cells throughout "your" body. Stranger still, the efficiency of this digestion process will depend in part on how you *feel* about spinach. It will digest better if you like it. Soon, in any case, the spinach that was "not-me" will be "me" when some of its mineral content is stored in your liver—assuming you identify with your liver. Which raises another interesting point.

Gordon Allport (who edited an often used modern edition of James's *Psychology*) gives an example.[14] Saliva in your mouth is "me." Spit it into a glass and, presto (yuk), it is no longer "me." This sort of oddity can be extended much further. Imagine pieces of your body removed from you by various misfortunes. Imagine that even your vital organs are replaced, one by one, with bits and pieces of mechanical wizardry or transplants from other bodies. Let's even imagine that we figure out how to transplant neurons one by one until your brain is made up of somebody else's neurons. Now ask yourself, In what sense is your self your body? Where is the boundary between "self" and "not-self" you have always taken for granted?

You may think this example far-fetched, but it isn't, really. There is not a molecule or atom in your body right now that was present in it a few years ago. Indeed, the atoms in your body are "exchanged" for alternative atoms much, much faster than that. What is retained, it seems, is only the pattern, the arrangement of energy and information. The idea of you. And your consciousness. If you think you are your body, as Deepak Chopra comments, you will have to ask yourself, Which body? When?[15]

Here is the point and the paradox (for human reality is spun of paradox). Not only your body but also your consciousness is a part of a web of energy and information connections. By actual calculation, some of the atoms in your body were in Jesus' body, others were "used" by Attila the Hun. Strange as it seems, there is no clear and definable boundary between your body and mine and even the Andromeda galaxy. As we have learned from modern physics, everything is connected to everything everywhere in what is sometimes called a "unified field."

The self, not-self paradox continues when we consider the nature of consciousness. When you have happy thoughts, your body will automatically produce "happy" molecules. When you wish to observe an atomic particle, like a proton, the proton will respond by being a "particle" for your observing instruments. (Subatomic particles act like waves, like ripples in a pond, when they aren't acting like "particles," and are not "things" at all.)

When you set up your canvas to paint a red landscape, the red colors will enter your consciousness, your experience. You may respond by adding a little blue. The new colors change your consciousness of your painting. And so on and on.

So where is the boundary between consciousness and the objective world? The answer is very strange. It is in our consciousness. And what does that mean? Ultimately, if one considers all that we know of relativity, quantum physics, chaos theory, and systems thinking, the conclusion must be that consciousness is not simply "something in your head," but a property of the universe. Indeed, it is just as likely that instead of consciousness being a by-product of matter, matter is a by-product of consciousness.[16]

We can see that the self, not-self paradox is profound and strange, not unlike consciousness itself. However, since we will use the expressions "self" and "not-self" throughout this book, here is a mental "handle" for keeping the two terms sorted out and reasonably meaningful.

Let the term "self" stand for a local part of the universe with which we identify.

Let the term "not-self" stand for any part of the universe that is experienced (directly or indirectly) but that is not identified as included in the "self."

Remember, however, that our "self" can only exist at all because we make a boundary between it and the "not-self" part of our world. The two poles of our experience, self and not-self, are a complementarity, like yin and yang. Because they are a complementarity, your self and your not-self are actually part of a unified whole.

The universe is only separable into distinct, disconnected parts by consciousness. But these divisions are largely arbitrary, and, ultimately, because everything everywhere is connected in a field of energy and information, they are only "real" while we experience them.

Finally, the relationship of the self and the not-self and the relationships of the two modes of knowing have the same nature. Both are complementarities. Light acts like particles if observed in one way and as waves when observed in another. It is not one or the other, it is both. That is the basic property of a complementarity. In the same way, the direct knowing of the heart, of the poet or the mystic, makes objective knowing uncertain and vice versa. Yet full knowing is both objective and relational.

Just as we may see the world by making it an object to our consciousness or by entering into relationship with it, consciousness may view reality from the perspective of the self or of the not-self. And just as in the case of the two modes of knowing, the two frames of reference appear to exclude each other. But this appearance, strange as it may seem, is an illusion. The Self, that which we are, is both self and not-self because we are part and whole. Both. Arthur Koestler coined the term "holon" to express this profoundly important idea.[17] You exist as a self precisely because of how that self exists in relationship to everything that is not-self. But this relationship is integral. Traditional spiritual sources state the matter unequivocally in a single remarkable declaration: There is nothing outside of you.

For those of us making our home in a consciousness state where this seems utterly impossible, the mystical declaration seems quite beyond our grasp. But we can, at least, sense this: What we experience, at every level of awareness (conscious or unconscious) is the equivalent of the perceived (and arbitrary) boundary of the self *at a particular level or frequency of conscious-*

ness. Your sense of self is not the same while you are dreaming, filing your taxes, or transported to a sense of oneness with the universe during meditation. In any case, a rock or a galaxy exists for you precisely because they are in your experience.[18]

The beauty of a meadow under fresh snow exists for you as an aspect of your self as experiencer. Your love for another exists because love is the energy of relating and that which we experience—however we name it—is the relationship itself.

THE GENERAL FORM OF THE BRENDEN MATRIX

The relationship between the complementarities of the two ways of knowing and the division of our experience between the self and the not-self gives us the general form called the Brenden Matrix.

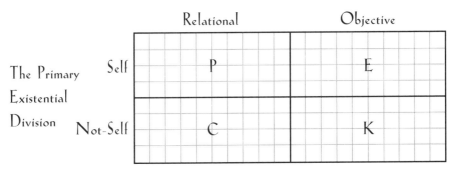

FIGURE 8: THE GENERAL FORM OF THE BRENDEN MATRIX

The Two Modes of Knowing

The symbols in each cell are like place holders or unknowns in a general equation of human consciousness and experience. When any fourfold model or typology is found to fit in the matrix, we will call it a matrix set.

31

Matrix sets may be discovered and nested in the Brenden Matrix at different levels of analysis, at different frames of reference. The four core needs are a Brenden Matrix set at the psychological level. But matrix sets with the same geometry and internal grammar (the same rules of relationship between quadrants) apply to our personal psychology, to the patterns of our relationships with others, and to the patterns we find in societies. This property of matrix sets is a very important one for matrix theory.

In Figure 9, we nest Carl Jung's four psychic functions in the Brenden Matrix. Taking a few moments to think about these functions in terms of the complementarities of the relational and objective modes of knowing and the existential division between self and not-self can help give you a feeling for how the matrix works.

Feeling (relational self or P quadrant) is the self-in-relationship. What we feel is at the heart of personal meaning. P may be thought of as representing our fundamental psychological nature, our psyche. Our psyche is also where we feel experience.

Thinking (objective self or E quadrant) is consciousness standing back to name and categorize. Thinking of the self makes the self an object to our consciousness. E here stands for "ethos" and refers to the rules for thinking we find in different cultures, using different languages.

Sensation (objective not-self, the K quadrant) seems to come from outside consciousness. Heat, pain, pleasure are objective to our awareness of them. Even the body as the receiver of sensation is always objective to our awareness. K stands for the Greek "chronos," a word for time, since sensations are aspects of our experience of space-time.

Intuition (relational not-self, the C quadrant) seems to come from within, just as sensation seems to come from outside. But intuition, hunches, inspirations arrive from somewhere else, from a not-self place that shows us, sometimes gently, sometimes with rude abruptness, relationships we had not seen. C may be thought of as standing for the Greek "cosmos"—referring to the entire universe, visible and invisible, which is, ultimately, where we are.

FIGURE 9: JUNG'S PSYCHIC FUNCTION AS A
BRENDEN MATRIX SET

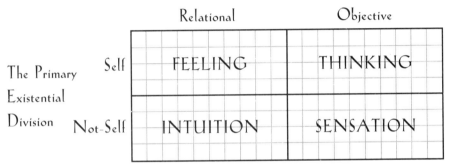

THREE RELATED MATRIX SETS

In Figure 10, three matrix sets are nested, gathering together three fourfold typologies from three frames of reference, three levels of analysis. Thinking about how these three matrix sets fit together offers a quick insight into what uses matrix theory may have for the human sciences.

The core needs (for giving and receiving love, for social identity, for nurturing and protecting the body, and for cosmic grounding) will stand for a psychological aspect of human nature. They should not need further explanation at this point. Four forms of human relations will stand for a social-psychological level, the level at which you and I interact. Four functions every human society must attend to in order to survive will stand for the sociocultural level of analysis.

FIGURE 10: THREE BRENDEN MATRIX SETS AT THREE LEVELS OF
ANALYSIS: PSYCHOLOGICAL, SOCIAL-PSYCHOLOGICAL, AND
SOCIOCULTURAL

Mode of Knowing

	Relational	Objective
Self	Love Needs Communal Sharing INTEGRATION (Family)	Social Identity Authority Ranking GOAL ATTAINMENT (State)
Not-Self	Cosmic Grounding Equity Matching LATENCY (Religion)	Body Needs Market Pricing ADAPTATION (Economy)

The Primary
Existential
Division

It should be understood that each of these levels of analysis has its own domain. What you think when you are sitting by yourself is not like what you think when you are conversing with a friend. The interaction creates a different kind of thing, which is dependent on the interaction. A social world, the system made up of all sorts of interactions organized by shared language, customs, and beliefs, is another thing, a structure with its own identity and rules. Rules of psychology are not the rules of people interacting, and the rules of whole societies or cultures are, once again, not like either of these.

Through an ambitious cross-cultural analysis, anthropologist Alan Fiske discovered four forms or models of human social relations.[19] In any social situation, we will "select" one of these as appropriate.

Fiske's four forms of social relations need almost no explanation in the context of the core needs (although his work deserves very serious attention if you are involved in the human sciences). The type of social relations he calls "equity matching" may be thought of in terms of universals, or transcendent principles applying to human relations, as in "All men are created equal" or "We are all children of God." We interact with each other this way when we vote in an election or try to make sure all students in a school are treated with equal fairness. Interacting with each other in terms of ideas about relative values of commodities—*market pricing*—goes back to Adam Smith's insistence that we humans are inclined to trade and barter. Its relationship to economic and adaptive activity is pretty obvious. "Authority ranking" refers to the ranking of social roles related to differences in power and privilege. A worker talking with his foreman will employ this sort of model for interaction—if he wants to keep his job. The category of social relations he calls "communal sharing" should not need much explanation. It is the way mothers act with their children, the way a Lakota warrior shares game with his kinship group.

The sociocultural level (the level at which a culture is expressed in the day-to-day behaviors we find in a society) nests sociologist Talcott Parsons's four functional requisites for any society.[20]

"Adaptation" means survival in a habitat; it has to do with economic activity, from subsistence horticulture to the manufacture of widgets. "Integration" means, roughly, getting along, and Parsons associates this functional requisite with communal groups, especially kinship systems, as well as with norms of cooperation. "Goal attainment" refers to getting things done as a group and involves deciding who gets to decide. This domain always has to do with hierarchical ranking and what might be called the power problem that always arises in a human group when there are differences of opinion. The "latency function" for Parsons is a bit obscure in some ways but refers to his idea that social systems are ordered by cultural norms, beliefs, and values. A term we may use in referring to this function is "legitimation." For example, why we get married, build houses a certain way, grow and harvest yams using special yam incantations, or punish thieves by cutting off their hands requires an overarching story, a mythology, cosmology, or theology that legitimates our customs and beliefs. A typical institution for legitimating a social world is religion.

It can be seen that these typologies are convergent, that they speak to something similar but at different levels of analysis.

While Fiske is obviously aware of the general fourfold structuring of human behavior, Parsons may not have been; he derived his model from a general effort to comprehend how societies are structured in terms of the functions of roles, norms, and institutions, and, in his later work, treated his functional requisites hierarchically. I've added a characteristic or primary social institution associated with each of Parsons's functional requisites.

It is the convergence of the model of four elemental core needs, along with the matrix sets derived from Fiske, Parsons, and Jung's four psychic functions, that gives rise to the basic hypothesis of matrix theory.

Human action and human social productions are systematically patterned by four universal core needs.

In practical terms, this means that human action, what you and I do all day, what we imagine, deny, intend, and desire, is about our core needs.

Human action is always informed by effective or ineffective, conscious or unconscious core-need strategies.

For the human sciences, the ramifications of these two hypotheses, taken in the context of the manner in which the matrix categories for any set interact, are complex and far-reaching. Matrix theory provides insight into patterns of social roles, sociocultural evolution, the forms and relationships of institutions like family, economy, or religion, the relationship of mechanisms of social control to human expression, the dynamics of socialization, the nature of deviance, the nature of cultural synergy (how well social institutions work together), and the dynamics of social change, to name some of the important ones. In short, for human scientists, matrix theory is a general, unifying model.

Matrix theory is also science in a different key; it declares once and for all that human science that ignores the breadth and depth of human experience is crippled at the outset. The methods of sociology and psychology are not, and cannot be, the methods of physics. On the other hand, what we may learn from the Brenden Matrix is not mythology, either. The method for making sense of its premises and models requires us to accept or reject its concepts in terms of concrete experience. In effect, it draws on a method that William James called "radical empiricism."[21] James suggests that we honor both our inner experience and our sensory experience, attempting to see how they complement each other in terms of pragmatic outcomes.

Eating disorders, for example, involve ineffective core-need strategies. Roughly, eating may become a substitute for giving and receiving love (which, as we shall see in later chapters, is not felt to be deserved in the first place). At the same time, not-eating becomes a substitute for getting the social identity and approval we need. Becoming aware of the actual, inner experience, the thoughts and feelings and associations accompanying binge eating, compulsive dieting, or purging, might empower the sufferer. She may become aware of what she really wants (love, social identity) and experiment with more authentic need strategies. But without attention to outer sensation (glossy magazine ads, television commercials, and so on, ad nauseam) and learning to re-interpret (or release) these images as virtually meaningless, a desirable, pragmatic outcome (eating when one is hungry and enjoying food) is less likely.

Matrix theory is imminently practical. It is not philosophy, nor is it ideology. It is not a system of beliefs. It is a guide to making human choices in terms of an empirical and pragmatic model of human needs. The Brenden Matrix is not Truth, but it may, indeed, be a compass to help us find ways to understand who we are. You might say matrix theory is a song for Socrates, who taught us that the unexamined life is not worth living. Ultimately, for the human scientist or the nonspecialist, that's what the Brenden Matrix and the theory surrounding it are for.

What the Brenden Matrix Isn't

At a profound level, the tendency of human mind-consciousness to perceive and arrive at fourfold models of human experience is about something basic in the nature of the human mind itself. The Brenden Matrix represents what I call an "ontomorph," a being form. Other representations of ontomorphs include the circle or mandala, and various representations of duality, like the famous yin-yang symbol of Taoism (which is complementarity within wholeness represented by the circle or mandala form). There are also trinities, like those abundant in Celtic symbolism, and the helix, or spiral, honored in many cultures, often represented by a symbol called the labyrinth. So it should not be imagined that everything important about human experience can be explained in neat fourfold boxes. The Brenden Matrix is only a map, even if it is, indeed, a very basic one.

Eventually, perhaps, an expanding vision for the human sciences will begin to incorporate understandings of other ontomorphs like the mandala or the helix into subtle and powerful guides to the relational order of the cosmos and our place in it.

The nineteenth-century poet and mystic William Blake was acutely aware of the cost of cold rationality and turning away from inner, relational knowing. In the poem addressed to Thomas Butts that heads this chapter, he called our abandonment of the timeless dimensions of the soul, of relational mode knowing, "Single vision." He called our entrancement with left-brained, mathematical models of the world "Newton's sleep," recognizing Isaac Newton's immense impact on the mentality of Western culture.

This book is about our core needs, their fourfold structure, and the journey to self-awareness. But it is also about how to hear the alarms being sounded by crime rates and divorce rates, by burning rain forests and global warming, by the restless longing of souls in pain all over this planet. For, if we will hear them, these are the alarms trying to wake us from "Single vision and Newton's sleep."

Intermezzo

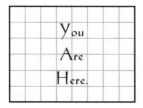

The previous chapter is full of intellectual constructs.

That is because we live in a culture of concepts, and thoughtful people are full of thoughts. Thoughts and thinking are the way we imagine we control the world. Therefore, balancing head and heart means honoring both thinking and knowing. Until we know. Then, perhaps, we will finally understand what thinking is for.

In this chapter there are tools of relational knowing that are for making practical sense of the intellectual models, the web of ideas called matrix theory, particularly that fourfold analytical gadget we call the Brenden Matrix.

Here are the tools: Paying attention to what's around you without judgment. Paying attention to what you want and what you are actually experiencing without judgment. Together these may be called self-honesty.

Here are the three principles of consciousness transformation that allow us to make the journey from the ego to the self. They allow us to use the mystery of four to change our lives.

Nonjudgment
Harmlessness
Forgiveness

If you know these to be spiritual principles and the idea of things spiritual makes you uncomfortable, make up a new way of thinking about them. They are techniques for leaving paradox and discovering what we want. Learning to use them produces real effects, unlike dieting, for example, which usually produces no effects. That should encourage us. Perhaps we can put a list of the principles under refrigerator magnets next to grocery lists and the soccer schedule.

Spiritual work is easier than dieting and has lasting effects.

3

What to Do with a Brenden Matrix

Today I have got out of all trouble, or rather I have cast out all trouble, for it was not outside, but within, in my opinions.

Marcus Aurelius

You've had a tour through some of the basic ideas of matrix theory. But beyond the curious fact that people often produce fourfold models of things, you may, in all fairness, ask what all this means in practical terms. So, before exploring what the Brenden Matrix can tell us about why you and I act the way we do, what social roles are all about, where our society seems to be headed, and why all of these things are connected, we may need some encouragement. You might like to know why you should care about anything with so esoteric a name as matrix theory.

Actually, the answer to that is simple enough. Properly understood, the Brenden Matrix is a sort of life compass. It is no accident that its basic form, represented, for example, in the symbol of the cross, is so deeply imbedded in our consciousness. If you are one of those who grasp its powers, you will find uses for it. It is a guide for choosing. Since you may not quite believe that, this chapter is meant to give you some hints about why this is so. It also suggests a few more tools for using the Brenden Matrix as a guide to the vital core needs beneath our restless longings.

Self-Honesty

Our behavior is rooted in our core needs. We are always in search of love, however ineffectively; we are perpetually working to construct and maintain a sense of identity in our social world; we devote lots of energy every day to body nurturance and survival needs. Finally, even if we do not carry the process in awareness, beyond the effort to construct and maintain a sense of self we probe continually to answer a question once posed by Albert Einstein. When he was asked in an interview what he thought was the most important problem facing mankind, he answered, "Is the universe friendly?" At some level of awareness, we need to sense that the universe has a place for us; we want to know if "the universe is friendly."

When we understand that everything we do is an effort to meet our core needs, we cross a threshold. Stepping over the threshold, beginning to pay attention to our emotions, our thoughts, the patterns of our life, we can begin to see the unique ways our life expresses itself against that benchmark. We all have the same core needs, but we have unique ways of trying to meet those needs. What each of us finds in life is different, but we share a common goal. Each of us must become aware of his or her deepest needs in order to pursue need strategies that will fulfill life and give it meaning.

We have two kinds of challenges in this quest.

THE FIRST CHALLENGE

To glimpse who we are, to begin to have some sense of the meanings and patterns of our lives, we must come to see how we are asleep to our deepest selves and their nature.

The only path to that goal is persistent, habitual, and utter *self-honesty*. Self-honesty is also a basic tool for making use of the Brenden Matrix.

We can't keep our hatreds and our thoughtless prejudices in some musty psychic attic, pretending they are not part of the experiences we are making for ourselves. We cannot pretend that our secret sexual fantasies are in one psychic room while our moments of emotional and physical intimacy with our spouses or lovers are in another place.

Self-honesty has many dimensions, but at least two disciplines are helpful in attaining it. Both of them have the same substance: paying attention.

OBJECTIVE PRESENCE

Paying attention to the objective world is what is required of visual artists, but, in one sense, we are the "artists" of our life experiences, so you don't have to be Vincent Van Gogh to practice objective presence. According to one story, Andrew Wyeth, the American painter, spent many hours astride the roof of a barn studying the reflections in the glass insulator globe of a lightning rod. He wanted to see what was there under shifting light, drifting clouds, bright sun, and evening twilight. The philosopher Edmund Husserl taught a technique for paying attention he called "eidetic reduction." For all its subtleties and ramifications, it is about seeing what is there, in the world around us or within our minds, with as little preconception as possible.

You'll find your own ways for practicing objective presence.

All that is required is a relaxed, even playful, effort to see without judgment. I find myself withdrawing judgment and "seeing what is there" by allowing myself to escape for a while into the wonderful Appalachian landscapes around my home. I also enjoy candlelight in the evening quiet, or simply being still for a few moments with one of the mineral specimens I've collected since I was very young. Sometimes I just pay attention to my cat.

Objective presence allows us to practice nonjudgmental awareness more easily than inner presence. Our egos are not as involved. Such pleasant exercises are also a simple form of "meditation" for people from Western cultures (who are not used to sitting still for long), as well as a way of experiencing the awareness of beauty that is part of our ground state, our natural self.

If you are lucky (or persistent), practicing objective presence is also a simple way to become aware of the "light" around things, which, apparently, represents the life energy throughout the cosmos. The first time I noticed vibrant, white halos was around ministers during church sermons. I would drift away from the substance of the preacher's words, and my eyes would go into a detached, relaxed focus. When I was younger, I wondered if what I was seeing was really there or simply some form of optical illusion. (There is a dark-light-contrast optical illusion of this sort.) I wondered whether or not it had to do with religion and churches. In time, however, I discovered I could see or "sense" this sort of light-energy field effect around people—usually when I was not looking for it—under a variety of conditions. It "flares," I've noticed, when people are speaking—giving out energy perhaps—and recedes when people are passive or "in-turned." Some people report that they can see these "auras" around people quite clearly, even distinguishing distinct patterns of color.

Being aware of the light energy around all things requires some practice, and it is a special kind of awareness in itself. I'm not very good at it myself. In any case, don't worry much about trying to see what you cannot. The key to objective presence is playful quietness, accepting the grace of the beauty around you. Let it be effortless. See what you see. Don't pretend not to see what you see. Pay attention.

INNER PRESENCE

Paying attention to your actual inner experience is like objective presence in a way, but it's trickier because our preconceptions, especially those that form around our egos in defensive patterns, are more likely to get in the way.

Practicing inner presence is, I suppose, the ultimate scientific method in the quest for the self. If your experience is like mine, you'll discover, by working at it a little bit or, more precisely, by letting it happen, lots of odd things that "don't fit."

Roughly, the landscapes of inner presence are any and all psychic or consciousness states you find yourself in, awake, drowsing, meditating, dreaming—or elsewhere. Sharing our inner presence with each other, by the way, is the heart of intimacy, and certainly among the kindest gifts we can bestow on each other.

What you will find through inner presence is what you will find. It need not be what someone else will find—even though there's lots of evidence that our experiences are more similar than we imagine. Inner presence can mean being a witness to your thoughts or emotions, watching them as you would a dragonfly's dance over water, a summer storm, or a desert sunset. It can also mean accepting anomalies. I once dreamed of having a Jeep make a right turn suddenly into the bike I was riding. Later, the accident happened. I remembered the dream in the instant that the Jeep ran into my bicycle. I couldn't prevent the accident, but I had a lesson in the nature of consciousness. Anomalies can be informative.

What you will find by paying attention to your inner experience will probably include odds and ends—odd things that have their own ends in our quest for the self. For years, out of my interest in things scientific, I've watched the endless disputes over whether or not there is such a thing as extrasensory perception. Mostly these are hot disputes over experimental design and statistical validity that would bore anyone who is not a determined researcher. Meanwhile, I've had dreams of things that didn't happen until later, "known" what would happen a little bit ahead in time, "known" who was on the phone before I picked it up, and had an unsought, out-of-body experience that taught me that I don't need my body to see, hear, and think. I've experienced so many "meaningful coincidences" that I could not possibly recount all of them. They range from opening a book at random to exactly what I was looking for to "chance" encounters with particular people, to learning to detect (increasingly obvious) patterns of synchronicity in my life course.

I've discovered that similar experiences are very common among us humans. And there is even some pretty good research data confirming this. In any case, learning to be present—to pay attention to what is outside of us or within us—is the elemental method for self-discovery. It is also, as we've said, the heart of intimacy. To share one's presence with another is a gift; to be with the presence of another is a gift. To enter into a space of joined presence is the greatest gift one may have and give—for in such sacred spaces there is no difference between having and giving. As Deepak Chopra has noted, what we find through intimacy, ultimately, is the self.[1] And the self is what connects us to each other and to our Source.

THE SECOND CHALLENGE

As you practice objective and inner presence, the four core needs may become more evident to you, and the substance of the second challenge emerges.

As we begin to glimpse the self at the core of our experience, we will begin to detect patterns. I do not need to prove this to you; you need to prove it to yourself. Among the patterns we find are the relationships that exist between our needs. The built-in intelligence of the Brenden Matrix can help us make sense of these patterns.

Although we will go into more detail about the relationships among our core needs in the pages ahead, here's an example. Our intuition and thinking functions must work together, or our knowing is partial and misleading. This is so even though one of these functions is focused in objective knowing and the other in the relational mode. The two functions may seem to be opposed and contradictory—even to exclude each other. The phone rings and you "know" who is calling. Intuition at work. Then you remind yourself that you cannot "know" who is calling until you pick up the phone. The objective mode has kicked in. You pick up the phone. It turns out to be who you "knew" was calling— Aunt Susan—whom you have not heard from for months. One part of your mind sees this sort of precognition as meaningful; another part wants to attribute it to mere coincidence. In short, the two functions—intuition and thinking—are related as an apparently paradoxical complementarity.

Here is the pattern of such conflicts. The core need associated with thinking is our need for social identity. But the social-identity core need is also our primary connection to our social world. A problem arises out of this fact. You want approval in your social world—which also amounts to self-approval—and part of your social conditioning includes norms of rationality, norms about thinking, which "rational and sensible" people are supposed to take for granted. You have been taught that you cannot know who is on the phone before you pick it up. To maintain your sense of allegiance to your consensus world, and thus to defend your sense of your identity, you will endorse that idea—even if it conflicts with your experience. We all do this.

In a documentary film, I saw two Amazonian Indians brought to a river bank by an anthropologist to witness the arrival and landing of a small airplane equipped with pontoons. The Indian women were in "reality shock." The category "airplane" did not exist in their consensus reality. One woman reacted by intermittently looking at the aircraft and turning her head away in disbelief. As she did this, she wiped her hand across her eyes as if to clear away a hallucination. We do not want to see what we do not believe can exist; we do not want to believe what we are not "supposed" to believe.

On the other hand, our desire to "think correctly" in order to gain self-approval and identity in a social world is only half the conflict in our example of Aunt Susan's phone call. Our intuition, the part of us that sees something meaningful about knowing that Aunt Susan is on the phone before we pick it up, is associated with our need for cosmic grounding. Part of us wants to feel, to believe, that such events are more than coincidence. Part of us wants to accept the experience for what it is.

Now, we may see that through inner presence we allow ourselves a choice. By tolerating paradox, we can see the phone experience with Aunt Susan as meaningful *and* we can think about it coherently. In doing that, we are choosing through an expanded awareness. We sense not only our need for social identity with its attendant conditioning about rules of rational thought, but also our genuine need for cosmic grounding, for knowing that we have a *meaningful* relationship to the cosmos.

The example may seem a trivial one, but it is in just this way, through paying attention to the balance of our deepest needs, that we can make meaningful choices. We may know that we can "know" what we cannot understand, even as we honor what we can comprehend within the limits of rational and logical thought. We can confront paradox and make such choices. When we do, the meanings of our lives begin to unfold around us. They may not be what we expect.

Three Laws of Consciousness Transformation

Practicing objective and inner presence in the pursuit of self-honesty is a technique that helps us discover the nameless self.

But I have found it helpful to place these practices in a context. For however we think of it, the quest for self-knowledge is a spiritual quest—that is, a quest for the ground at the foundation of our existing. Put another way, a spiritual path is necessary to self-knowledge, just as self-knowledge is necessary to the awareness of our core needs and the fulfillment of our nature. I'm not sure that it matters what the spiritual path is called—or even if one calls it a "spiritual path." It may or may not be associated with a spiritual tradition, with organized religion, or with any sort of religious orthodoxy. That is so because, ultimately, what one is about is becoming aware of one's actual, concrete experience. The preconceptions of systems of belief, of dogmatic assumptions, may actually hinder that process.

In any case, there are three principles that, in fact, are techniques or disciplines required for effective self-honesty: nonjudgment, harmlessness, and forgiveness. The principles are well known. In fact they are recognizable at the heart of every major spiritual tradition.[2]

Nonjudgment

In practical terms, practicing objective or inner presence is, simply, exercising nonjudgment. It is necessary to self-honesty, even if it means practicing inner presence with regard to our judgments! Typically, to be sure, we say we are critical of people who are "judgmental," but, in fact, we are actually only observing that people who attack others may make us uncomfortable.

Nonjudgment is not about not having judgments. We must estimate the distance to a stop sign in order to brake our car; we must estimate our sense of another's honesty; we cannot avoid judging chocolate as preferable to vanilla if we like chocolate.

Nonjudgment is about our consciousness of our judgments and the meaning we ascribe to them. It has components. (1) We cannot know the overall meaning of the things that happen in our lives. We must learn that; it can be a hard lesson. (2) We cannot be sure that our evaluations of the sensory world are valid. That is also hard to deal with, but releasing the meanings we attribute to appearances can also be quite calming. (3) Most important, perhaps, we can intend and we can attempt to see through appearance. Mainly, this means we can choose to seek the natural self—the energies of who we are, of what we desire— in another. That is one of the utilities of grasping the universal nature of our core needs. Everyone you have met or ever will meet needs to give and receive love. We can choose to see through postures of defense or attack. In this way we can choose to seek the natural self in our own actions. If that last declaration seems puzzling, bear with me. What we mean by this notion of a "natural self" will be explored in the next chapter.

HARMLESSNESS

Harmlessness is surrendering our ego defenses; its objective is to discover that no defenses are needed. The objective is difficult to attain since our social worlds—especially in Western culture— are mainly about defending, attacking, and competing.

Harmlessness—turning the other cheek, giving up attack in our thoughts and attitudes—is mainly learning about our ego and its relationship to the self. We will see how the Brenden Matrix permits us some insight into this relationship in the next chapter, but the principle is simple enough. The ego we invent to define ourselves and to find a place in our social world is, by its nature, a fortress for defense and attack. Learning harmlessness is finding enough security in the self to allow us to sidestep the ego's stratagems.

FORGIVENESS

Nothing seems more difficult than forgiveness. But it is a principle of self-awareness. A difficult principle. Holding grievances against people (or against ourselves) is a powerfully attractive strategy for explaining to ourselves why we experience pain and confusion. It is a strategy our egos are busy attending to nearly all the time. In fact, as far as I can tell, forgiveness is nearly impossible while we are in ordinary awareness. We cannot forgive out of the same consciousness in which we assign blame.

It has been helpful to me to think of forgiveness as a two-edged sword, a remarkable Excalibur that can only be drawn from the stone out of a consciousness state that is not normally familiar to us. One edge of the sword-that-heals lies in the nature of time; the other is planted in the timelessness of non-judgment.

All our ascriptions of blame, all the hurts we nurture in our mind, occur in imaginary time. Yes, imaginary time. Your father's verbal abuse, robbing you of self-esteem, happened when you were young; your hurt is carried in your mind. Now. The time of an abusive event does not exist in space-time; it is a content of our conditioned memory. Once, I employed age-regression hypnosis with a friend. She had attended a Catholic school and harbored a painful memory of being coldly ignored by one of the teaching nuns. In the age regression, this person discovered that the nun had, in fact, been paying attention to something else in the classroom, not ignoring her. Of course, that does not mean that actual abuses or attacks by others do not occur; it does suggest that our definition of them may not be what we carry around in our minds. That can be a helpful insight.

It is also helpful to understand that just as our transgressions against others are ill-conceived efforts to meet our core needs, so are those of whoever may transgress against us.

More important, we can discover that the location of our hurt is not in the past, but in our minds. You can choose to release a trauma because it is in *your* mind. And one technique of releasing has the same property as paying attention. It is possible to discover that after accepting and entering into the meaning of a past trauma, you are still you. You are not the trauma. You are not the effects you have accepted from it. That is a threshold of forgiveness.

The fullness of forgiveness, on the other hand, seems to arrive in knowing all of these insights at once. To forgive is to receive the grace of expanded awareness and may well be experienced as transcendent intervention from something beyond the sense of self.

You may wonder at what seems a sudden leap in this chapter from fairly abstract theoretical ideas to a discussion of things that hover somewhere between dreams and the occasional bright glimpses we may have that whisper in the light. But remember, the practical purposes of matrix theory are about seeing things whole—with rationality and with the heart. The tools for making use of the Brenden Matrix are, ultimately, the ways of discovering the self. And inner work, whether we call it our religion, our spiritual path, or something else, is imminently practical in that quest.

Spiritual work is not an escape from daily life, after all. It is a way of fulfilling what we do, moment by moment. To be mindful and still in meditation, in a monastic cell, or in the midst of a mass, may be helpful. But we must not imagine that things spiritual are to be set apart. The quest for the self is the quest for who we are in rush-hour traffic, while trying on shoes in the mall, while removing a boiling pot of green beans from a burner, while soothing the anguish of the seventh grader who forgot his math assignment. Spiritual work is not about escape, it is about transformation.

INTERMEZZO

The next chapter is about choosing. Choosing is not what we imagine it to be. We think we make plans and choices all the time. However, when you feel compelled, try paying attention to what happens to your plans. How many of them are actually only adaptive responses to conditions you were not aware of choosing? How many of your plans actually work out? If your plans do seem to work out, do they get you what you expected?

Do not consider these questions as judgments; think of them as koans, as riddles for meditation. The only meaningful answers to them occur in your actual experience.

Choosing is alignment. It is effortless. Choosing happens when what we want and what we need are known to be the same thing. When this happens, things actually change. Our lives change. Worlds change.

However, choosing does not happen in the ordinary consciousness of everyday life. What we call choosing is something like sorting. What we are doing when we imagine we are choosing is taking a path of least resistance, avoiding pain, seeking the pleasures guilt will allow. It is a muddled business, since we do not know the value of either our pleasures or our pains.

Choosing requires us to know the difference between the ego and the self. Our egos are who we imagine ourselves to be. Imaginary entities do not choose; they follow the rules we have made up for a game we do not understand and cannot win. The ego game is selflessly designed to assure that it must be lost. The roof of the ego is perception, its floor is death, its chambers are waiting rooms full of clamor and sterile silences. Macbeth said that life is "a tale told by an idiot, full of sound and fury, signifying nothing." It is not; but you cannot prove that out of ego consciousness.

We honor perception—our sensory awareness of the outer world—and make much of it; we know very little of inception—the way in which we may know the inner world—and we suffer for it. We imagine what we perceive to be outside of us when, in fact, it is inside of us. We imagine inception to be inside of us when, in fact, we are inside of it.

4

Choosing

The past and present wilt. . . .
I have filled them and emptied them,
And proceed to fill my next fold of the future.

Walt Whitman

We have four core needs: the need to give and receive love, to find a social identity in our social world, to nurture and protect the body, and to find cosmic grounding. So why are we often not in touch with these needs? Why, for example, do most of us confuse our social status or even the car we drive with our place in the universe? Why do we imagine that the spiritual dimension in us is a product of wishful thinking or the dreaminess of poets and mystics? Why do we have so much trouble integrating our desire, our life energy, with our feeling and intuition? Why, for example, are we more inclined to associate our life energy—Eros—with sin, rather than with our vitality?

Two concepts can help guide us to usable answers, and both of them can be summed up in this way: Social worlds are diligent in the fiendish task of splitting our consciousness into opposed warring camps. This happens in two ways.

First, social worlds have built into them a very strong tendency to endorse either the relational or the objective mode of knowing while devaluing its complement. Hopi culture, for example, is inclined to honor and to grasp the relational way of knowing. In Western culture, on the other hand, we have been strongly encouraged to enshrine objective-mode knowing as "the way" to know. What cannot be weighed and measured is not likely to be considered real and valuable. In fact, we are inclined to honor rationality and devalue direct, intuitive knowledge with a single, pejorative term: "mysticism."

Here we will call the tendency of human social worlds to endorse either relational or objective knowing the "psychosocial exclusion principle." The principle has the persistent effect of devaluing either our objective or our relational core needs, depending on the culture we live in. In Western culture, by devaluing the relational way of knowing, we devalue the relational core needs for giving and receiving love and for cosmic grounding. An effect of this has been the weakening of the social institutions associated with these core needs—family and religion.

The results of the exclusion principle can be devastating. In America, as many of us have become functionally illiterate in the languages of feeling and of intuition, families are left to float on precarious rafts in an ocean of state bureaucracies and profit-driven corporations. Even as we give lip service to "family values" we seem not to understand that the resources of a society must support communal groups (families, neighborhoods) because these are the heart of a society. At the same time, as religion is reduced to creeds and dogmas, direct relational (intuitive and spiritual) experiences are very often held suspect. In a very profound sense, neither our love needs nor our need for cosmic grounding is well understood.

Imagining we can see and know everything important through the objective way of knowing, science becomes scientism, a sort of ad hoc religion. Given our fear of death, medical science in particular becomes an "ultimate authority." In fact, a medical doctor inhabits a role much closer to the priest's role in earlier cultures than does a typical Protestant minister.

Second, socialization, the process by which we learn language and are inducted into a social world, produces another sort of split in us, that between the self and the ego. Although the general idea that we can be too "egoistic" is grasped, even in the "common sense" of our consensus reality, the actuality of what we may be beyond egoism is a mystery to us. The peculiar built-in intelligence of the Brenden Matrix provides some important insights into how this split works and what effects it has on our consciousness.

THE PSYCHOSOCIAL EXCLUSION PRINCIPLE

While the peculiar division of the relational and the objective, the whole and the part, is tangled through Western thought like crabgrass, it appears to have its effects in every culture. Roughly, indeed, cultures tend to fall into two general categories: they are either relational or objective. American society is an example of an objective-mode culture; Hopi Indian culture—to the extent that it has survived years of encroachment by the surrounding objective culture—is relational. Hopi see personal relations, relations to nature, causality, and the nature of time in ways that are alien to Western thinking.

How, precisely, the exclusion principle develops in a society is uncertain, but the complementarity property of the ways of knowing is probably at the heart of the matter. The knowing of a poem seems useless when we need to replace a light switch; the most elaborate technological explanation is driven from our minds like leaves in the wind when we confront the merry tumult of romantic love or the aching void of death.

Although the two ways of knowing, like yin and yang, are the faces of one thing, when we are focused in one mode, the other wavers like a mirage. Light beamed through a single slit scatters over a target screen as if we were spraying fine grains of sand through it. Light beamed through a double slit produces inter-ference patterns of the sort we get when two pebbles are tossed into a pond and their widening ripples intersect. We can choose how we will observe light. Apparently, with our own built-in uncertainty principle, we may also choose to focus our awareness in the relational or in the objective. We will see the fire or the rose—to borrow a famous line from T. S. Eliot—or, as in Figure 1, the faces or the vase.

Illustrations of this sort have often been used to demonstrate the manner in which the two modes of knowing appear to exclude each other. Notice in Figure 1 that you can see two faces or you can see a vase. Take your pick. Save through a silent, non-judgmental patience (which, in fact, looks through the appear-ance) you cannot see both at once. And that, in a graphic moment, is our built-in exclusion principle. In any perceptual act, we "translate" what we perceive in one mode or the other, but not both. When we are in the relational mode of knowing, the objective mode may appear superficial, brittle, and illusory. In the objective mode, the relational way of knowing may seem mystical, dreamy, impractical, and irrational.

Of course, as a practical matter, since we walk around with both hemispheres of our cerebrum, we are continually "processing" our world out of both modes. Language can be employed as a wrapping for either way of knowing, although it usually takes a poet to convey relational knowing.

Here is one of Robert Frost's shortest poems:

We dance round in a ring and suppose,
But the Secret sits in the middle and knows.

The poem illustrates, in a relational use of language, the antagonism between the two modes. Objective-mode knowing is always knowing at second hand, since it is dependent on signs and symbols, especially language. The word "rose" is not a rose. No elaborate description of the rose, its species, color, and biology will be our experience of it. We cannot get beyond Gertrude Stein's homily. To say "a rose is a rose is a rose" is still to tread on words and to suppose. Relational knowing, direct knowing, is the matrix, the womb of all knowing. But, in fact, the dialectic of supposing and knowing is the quality of human mentation. We dwell in the duality of the relational and the objective, and it is their dance, however conflicted, that we must deal with.

All of us deal all the time with this exclusion principle, with the "now you see it, now you don't" property of ordinary waking consciousness, in different ways. We wake from a dream, its imagery still immediate to our awareness. Coming back to ordinary waking consciousness, though, we wash out the imagery with a flood of inner verbiage, trying to "make sense of it," even as its direct feeling and meaning slip away from us. We have a "hunch" about another's feelings, then discount it because it is not "rational." The dance goes on and on; the center stays in the center.

I've written a bit of music. Almost always these modest musical efforts have had to do with the mood or quality of a stage play I was working on. Since my technical training as a musician ranks between thin and none, I become especially aware of the relational-objective dialogue involved in the process of musical composition. I don't know why one chord plays off another, why it's time for an arpeggio, where a melody comes from. In writing lyrics, I discover the remarkable thing that happens when a half note accompanies a word. Without intuition and feeling, no music happens. On the other hand, music is, in part, mathematically precise relationships between variations in pitch, tempo, and rhythm. If I don't attend to these relationships in the work of translating the music into notation, the music is only something in my head. If I don't become conscious of logical form (verse, chorus, verse, bridge, verse, chorus), the music will be "formless."

The dance of supposing and knowing will be associated with different ideas, norms, beliefs, and attitudes, depending on the social reality we live in. The structure of the language we use, tacit values, the organization of social roles—all of these things will tend to either encourage a balance between the modes of knowing or discourage one mode at the expense of the other.

Why human cultures have been mainly relational for most of our human history, evolving into left-brained forms only with the rise of urbanized civilizations, is uncertain. But cross-cultural and historical evidence supports the idea that the mode of production of a society, the arrangement of social roles around the way we produce and distribute economic resources, has a strong influence on how people think about the world and themselves.[1] In Westernized society, dominated by what I call Newton's triangle—materialism, objectivism, and determinism—the economy suffuses, dominates, overwhelms daily life. We have no temple complexes; we have shopping malls.

Preliterate cultures, on the other hand, from hunting-and-gathering bands through tribal levels of organization, seem all to have been relational.[2] Some of these cultures, like the Hopi of Arizona, manage to retain some of these "right-brained" qualities. Even after centuries of pressure from left-brained Western culture, the Hopi retain myth and ritual—relational mode knowing—at the center of their lives. Their way of making a living centers around the cultivation of corn in a desert environment—not a "practical" mode of production from the Western point of view. Yet it is precisely the nurturant relationship with the corn and with the living Earth—as well as with the spirit realm of the kachinas—that forms Hopi awareness.

Australian Aboriginal cultures, Native American cultures, African tribal cultures, all manifest patterns of mentality that are similar. In these social worlds, ideas about the nature of time and causality, the relationships of the social to the cosmic order, are radically unfamiliar to the modern, Western mind.

Apparently, the shift to objective-mode culture began to occur in various areas where urban civilization came into existence, beginning in the Middle East about 4000 B.C. From about 500 B.C. on, there were oscillations between relational and objective modalities of culture, especially in the Middle East and Europe.[3] But only in Europe did the peculiar confluence of cultural and historical conditions give rise to modern, corporate culture, which would come to dominate the planet. And Western culture is, by its premises and values, fiercely, tenaciously devoted to the objective mode of knowing. That fact is a powerful attractor, influencing your life and mine.

In simplest terms, the exclusion principle, built into social worlds, is like an immense magnet in its effects on our power to choose. It drags us toward the relational or the objective. In modern, corporate culture, the power with the left brain, rationality, and materialism. Therefore, automatically, inevitably, our understanding of our relational core needs for giving and receiving love and for cosmic grounding are devalued and misunderstood. At the same time, our needs for social identity and for meeting body needs are made elaborate and perplexing precisely because they are forced to compensate for flawed, muddled, and largely unconscious relational core-need strategies.

The great sociologist Max Weber named the primary force behind our Western world view "rationalization." He called it an "iron cage," which he linked to the secularization of religious insight, practical and applied science, capitalism, and our economic class system.[4] We have built a world view based on linear reason, linear time, rationality based in words and symbols, all of which is organized in terms of impersonal corporate and bureaucratic hierarchies of power and summed up in the notion of the "bottom line."

THE SELF AND THE EGO

The synchronies and asynchronies of choosing are experienced all the time in the conflicts of feeling, naming, sensing, and valuing. We feel attraction to a person whose social position is not appropriate to expressing that attraction. We fall in love with our fourth-grade teacher, for example, or we lust after a married coworker. Standing in the warm shower is sensually pleasant. But we may worry about dry skin, the electric bill for too much hot water, or, almost always, the rush to get to work. We love carrot cake, but not the calories we ascribe to it; we value hard work when our senses and feelings ache for a time of vegetative withdrawal. It is in the flow of actual consciousness that ordering—usually out of unconscious conditioning and habit—meets the chaos of choosing or, more often, blind, reflexive reaction.

The structure of our conflicted inner dialogues can be visualized using two matrix sets, one representing the self, the other the ego. To imagine this visualization, we must first conceive a difference between these two things—the self and the ego.

Fortunately, that can be done out of ordinary experiencing, especially if you are making an effort to practice objective or inner presence.

Here is a simple exercise that is familiar to anyone working on self-knowledge. Sit quietly and observe your thoughts. Do this until you recognize that the "I" that observes the thoughts isn't the thoughts. The observer, sometimes called the "silent witness," is a face of the self. Most of our thoughts aren't; they are ego speak.

Another exercise in awareness involves becoming conscious of what happens when you dream. We are present in a dream as an actor; we carry out little dramas in dream space. We also observe our action; we are an audience to the drama. Finally, most mysteriously, we are the dream producer. The dream producer is a face of our deeper consciousness, of the self. As a matter of fact, this trinity of consciousness is present in ordinary waking consciousness, too, and observing what happens around us as though it were a dream can be enlightening.

Sometimes simply becoming aware of the detached observer in us can draw us toward awareness of the self. In talking with a customer or scolding our four-year-old, we may "catch ourselves" playing a role. We "watch ourselves" making an impression for someone we've just met. A part of our consciousness "observes" the bodily business of making love, making coffee, putting on eye shadow.

THE FOURFOLD SELF

Just as the heart of our core needs is in the feeling function, in our need to give and receive love, the heart of our actual identity may be called the natural self. In his conception of the magical child, Joseph Chilton Pearce has told us a lot about the idea of a natural self, for being in touch with what is natural in us has a magical quality.[5] In terms of metaphoric or mythic thinking, the natural self can be represented by a pentagram.

FIGURE 2: THE FIVE DIMENSIONS OF THE NATURAL SELF

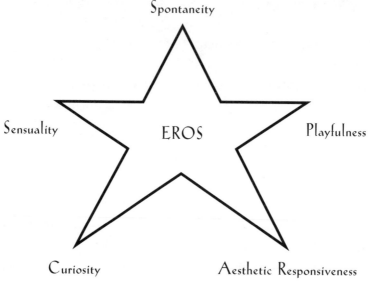

In the mythic system of numerology, five is the peculiarly human number; our primal ancestor may be the starfish nymph with its rudimentary notochord and bilateral symmetry. We have five-fingered hands. In any case, the natural self is sensuous, spontaneous, playful, curious, and responsive to beauty.

The center of our human qualities is Eros, the primal energy of desire, expression, extension, and projection. In Greek thought, Eros was considered the most ancient of the gods. In fact, Eros is the closest term we Westerners have for "life energy." In Chinese thought this same energy is called *chi*; in Hindu thought, it is called *prana*. It is the same thing, although different aspects of this primal energy are emphasized in the different traditions. We humans are erotic in our sensual and feeling nature, and that energy suffuses all our longing. Thwarted, repressed, or blocked, it becomes the energy of hatred, anger, fear, and cruelty.

When we allow it, the life energy of the magical child in us spreads out into our curiosity, our fascination and awe in the face of symmetries, synchronies, and beauty, into our playfulness, and into our moments of spontaneity. Spontaneity in the child, in our hidden child, is the quality of time in the natural self. It is present, without judgment, wide-eyed and alert.

The qualities of the natural self spill out into the other aspects of the self as well. We are sociable; we play together. We dwell in bodies full of the sensual. We are children in the light of over-arching consciousness, part of the aliveness of the cosmos itself, and, in this way, we are transcendent and timeless.

The facets of the self may be represented in a Brenden Matrix set like that given in Figure 3.

FIGURE 3: A BRENDEN MATRIX REPRESENTATION OF THE STRUCTURE OF THE SELF

The Modes of Knowing

		Relational	Objective
The Primary Existential Division	Self	NATURAL SELF	SOCIABLE SELF
	Not-Self	TRANSCENDENT SELF	BODY SELF

A way of thinking of the four faces of the self represented in Figure 3 is in terms of connections. Although all the aspects of the self are, in fact, part of us in every moment, in every decision or action we incline one face of the self toward whatever is happening. Yet, as we do that, every other aspect of the self appears and reappears in the context of that moment.

The natural self, for example, is our connection to psyche, to the heart of our being, to the soul. Yet, when we smile and look into another face with openness and curiosity, we are using the body to express the natural self. Indeed, the energy of Eros flows from the natural self into every other part of the self, even circulating in and out of the transcendent self, which is its Source. In the same way, however, our body states, our sociability, and the transcendent in us flows outward to the other shores of the self.

The sociable self is our connection to others, the body connects us to the biosphere and to the Earth, while the transcendent self connects us, from within, to the center of existence, which is the same for all expressions of life, everywhere.

The Self, our ultimate identity, is more than any representation we may make of it. But the Brenden Matrix guides us to understand that there are faces of the self related to our psychic functions and our core needs. Recognizing this is a step toward self-knowledge. It is also the beginning of a journey into uncertainty—and chaos. For to glimpse the dimensions of the self is also to recognize the extent of our numbness, our drowsy wandering in the trance of a social world. Part of recognizing illusion is dis-illusion.

The next step into disillusion, a consideration of the structure of the ego, can be troubling. A sense of humor helps.

THE EGO

Beginning with Freud, there are a number of ways to think of the nature of the psyche, but none unequivocally differentiates the self and the ego. Yet, if one conceives of the self as even a potential in us, often hidden, often unrecognized, often unfulfilled, it is possible to borrow concepts from Freud, Jung, and others to conceive of a constructed "self" which is not the self. We will use the time-honored term "ego" to designate this construction, mainly because the term—from the Latin "I"—is convenient and partly because the ego is where our waking consciousness tends to focus.

In Figure 4, you will see a Brenden Matrix set that is a model of the ego. If you will think of the terms in each cell of the table in relationship to the core needs and the psychic functions, the coherence of the model should be reasonably apparent. For simplicity, we've left out the designations of the primary existential division and the modes of knowing, since you will be familiar with these by now.

FIGURE 4: A BRENDEN MATRIX REPRESENTATION OF THE STRUCTURE OF THE EGO

	Relational	Objective
Self	SHADOW	MASK
Not-Self	SUPEREGO	BODY IMAGE

The terms "shadow" and "mask" are borrowed from Jung. But it should be understood that this model of the ego is a practical, not a theoretical, one. I am not attempting to revise Jung's analytical psychology. Instead, drawing on Jung's insights, I am suggesting a different frame of reference for the sake of pragmatic analysis.

In Jung's system of thought, the shadow, as an aspect of the personality, is thought of as an archetype with primeval roots in our evolutionary history. As such, it is both a source of our "instinctual nature" and of our "animal spirits." Like Freud's id, with its unruly libido, the shadow can be dangerous. It must be civilized by a socially acceptable persona (from the Latin, meaning "mask"). And, in Jungian thought, the persona, too, has an archetypal quality.

I do not deny underlying archetypal (collectively shared) qualities in either the shadow or the mask (persona). But I am distinguishing them from the underlying structure of the self. For what I call the natural self is the foundation, the underlying "instinctual nature," which is archetypal, while the shadow, certainly with deep roots in the unconscious and its own archetypal geography, tends to be its antagonist. It is an odd situation. We need the power of our shadow, for we store a lot of life energy there. But we must also work to get beyond the repressions, the denial, and the guilt that force the shadow out of our awareness. For, in effect, I am declaring with Anne Frank that "people are really good at heart."

The primary characteristic of the ego is that it is a structure of defense and attack. We use it to defend what needs no defense—the natural self—and it is, for practical purposes, the structure of our experiences of evil. What that means and what we may do about it will be considered as our discussion proceeds.

THE RELATIONSHIP OF THE EGO AND THE SELF

Perhaps the key practical problem of self-knowledge is distinguishing the natural self from the shadow. But it is also in understanding that the shadow is an effect of the socialization of the self. The shadow is not so much a structure as it is an absence of light. It is a shadow, indeed. And the shadow is cast by the mask, by the "ego ideal" we are required to invent in order to be acceptable in a social world. The mask is a "myth" about who we think we are or should be. At some level of consciousness we know the mask is an ideal, a sham, but we defend it, sometimes savagely. The ego's "ideal"—the fortress of the ego's precarious sense of "self-worth"—is what attempts to hide, suppress, and deny the magical child at the core of the self. As it does that it "casts a shadow."

Interestingly, too, our experience of being a body, framed as a body image trapped in time and change, casts a shadow on the superego. It encourages us to associate feelings of guilt and fear in the superego with the view of the body as a fragile, contingent part of the self, subject to sickness, injury, pain, and death. If I am bad, I—as a body—will deserve to be punished. Death becomes a penalty for sin and the ultimate expiation of guilt.

In the process called socialization, when we are inducted into a social world, we are abducted into a split consciousness and drawn away from the self. To survive, we learn to accommodate what is natural in us to the alien realm into which we are born. We learn to identify not with reality, but with a local consensus about reality. We are encouraged to conceal or abandon our roots in the self. We learn to categorize and order the world in terms of language and symbol; we learn how to act like a male or a female; we internalize the preconceptions and tacit assumptions around us. In short, we learn to identify with the ego.

Why?

In the simplest terms, we abandon the self in favor of the ego in an attempt to meet our core needs! The ego is the emperor of self-deception, raised to power over us by the inherent insecurities of living in a body in a human social world. We trade the natural self for the power of the shadow in order to be loved (which is one reason why what we call "love" may be about possession, submission, or domination). We trade our sociability for a mask of sociability in order to gain social identity and approval. We trade the natural grace of the body as a vehicle of expression for an anxiously perceived projection, a body image. To complete the scheme of self-annihilation, we trade the quiet center, the transcendent self, for the angry guilt and fear of internalized self-judgments—a superego.

We can visualize all of this in a useful way by considering the matrix sets of the self and the ego as two general aspects of our psychic nature. But in the illustration in Figure 5, there are some additional concepts to consider: perception, which seems to flow into consciousness from outside us, and inception, which flows from within.

FIGURE 5: THE RELATIONSHIP OF THE EGO AND THE SELF

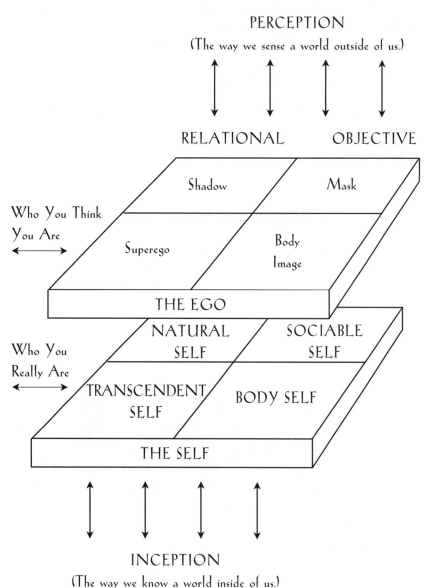

PERCEPTION

(The way we sense a world outside of us.)

RELATIONAL   OBJECTIVE

Shadow   Mask

Who You Think
You Are

Superego   Body
Image

THE EGO

NATURAL   SOCIABLE
SELF   SELF

Who You
Really Are

TRANSCENDENT   BODY SELF
SELF

THE SELF

INCEPTION

(The way we know a world inside of us.)

Identity, the sense of "I-am," may be understood in terms of dimensions or sources of knowing as well as in terms of modes of knowing and the fourfold structurings of consciousness. So while the main point of the illustration in Figure 5 is to represent how the structures of the ego correspond to those of the self, it is also to illustrate a few things about the nature and dynamics of our consciousness.

KEY IDEAS FROM FIGURE 5

1. First and foremost, please note that for each potential in the self, there is an antagonistic aspect of the ego. Thinking of the ego as a nearly opaque sheet of glass, we visualize how the shadow occludes the natural self, the body image the body, the mask our natural, playful sociability. In the same way, the superego, our internalized patterns of guilt, obscures our innocence, our transcendent nature.

2. "Above" the ego in this illustration we see the substance of the sensory realm, perception. We may think of perception as the dimension of objectivity. We see red, feel heat, taste salt, weigh ounces of silver. But, of course, in human social worlds perception is filtered through the subtle codings and preconceptions built into language—reflecting the assumptions, beliefs, and values of a culture—which includes the local effects of the psychosocial exclusion principle. Later on in this book, attempting to understand the trance induced in us by social worlds, we'll have more to say about language and perception. But most of us probably realize, for example, that if we speak English, we may not see the world quite the same way as we might if our native language were Navajo. What we may not realize beyond this is that what we perceive, what we see, taste, smell, and feel, is also conditioned by language to an amazing degree.

The ego is a filter between the realm of perception and the self. Conditioned perception is the structure of illusion.

3. From the foundation of the self and its ultimate Source there is what we may call "inception." By that term we refer partly to the dimension of the subjective, but also to more than that. Inception is the flow of information, of knowing, from within, mainly out of ordinary intuition and feeling, but sometimes out of direct knowing from more compelling and mysterious sources, such as the shaman's trance, near-death experiences, meditation, or contemplative prayer. The energy of inception attempts always to realign our perception with the relational matrix of knowing. Inception tries to undo the illusions of perception.

4. Given that perception is filtered through the ego and inception is structured for us by the potentials in the self, we may see that perception and inception may either complement or oppose each other. That is certainly what we experience. It is what is meant by the comment in Proverbs, "As he thinketh in his heart, so is he." It is a way of understanding why a fast ride on a motorcycle may be fun for one person and traumatic for another. It is a way of seeing why one person will die from the mere diagnosis of cancer while another will live for many years with the cancer, and still another will see the tumor vanish.

In the context of this model of some key "players" in our consciousness and experiencing, we may wonder where we might locate other fourfold structures we've discussed, like Jung's psychic functions or the core needs. That can be answered, at least approximately. The core needs may be thought of as inherent in the potential faces of the self. The psychic functions, on the other hand, might best be conceived as "sandwiched" between the ego and the self. Were the ego to vanish, along with the human experience as we presently conceive it, the psychic functions would collapse, undifferentiated, back into the potential of the self.

In fact, however, the psychic functions mediate between the self and the defensive structure of the ego, oscillating, so to speak, between their respective attractions. We may feel, think, sense, and intuit in terms of the ego or in terms of the self. It is important to understand that relational-mode knowing is not "correct" simply because it is relational, any more than an objective assessment that the Earth is flat is valid because it is based on objective observation.

Roughly, relational knowing is valid to the extent that it is in alignment with the self and evasive of the ego's defensive stratagems. Biased perception dwells in the nature of the ego. That bias may be "sure" that black skin is inferior to white skin in "objective" terms. On the other hand, the ego is also ambitious in its efforts to co-opt inception. It may interpret the vision of a saint as a demonic possession, cast a fearful, egoistic interpretation on a healer's touch, or see witchcraft in a precognitive dream.

The near-death experience illustrates the problem. As a side effect of modern medical technology, millions of people have reported near-death experiences, or NDEs.[6] Typically, these experiences involve leaving the body—observing it on an operating table, for example—then proceeding to a "realm of light" through a dark tunnel. Often the NDE will involve encounters with relatives who are deceased, a life review—sometimes offering a choice about returning to the body—and, not infrequently, interaction with a "being of light," who enfolds the person in peace and unconditional love. The typical NDE experiencer undergoes a variety of life changes after the experience, including a re-vision of ordinary reality and loss of the fear of death. (See Chapter 10 for further comments on NDEs.)

Quite simply, an NDE is a dramatic instance of inception. But the experience itself may or may not make it through the hedgerows of the consensus trance without considerable distortion. Often, people who have had these experiences are afraid to reveal them—for good reason. Some NDE survivors have been treated as psychotic and subjected to the violence of "therapy" involving psychotropic drugs and confinement in an institution. Others have struggled to reconcile their experiences to their pre-conceptions about reality, sometimes attempting to impose conventional religious ideas on what happened to them. Inception must always contend with perception.

Put another way, individuation, self-knowledge, is learning that our core needs are expressive of the nature of the self. What we truly want is who we are. That is why self-honesty is crucial in the quest for the self.

A bit whimsically, we may think of the balance of perception and inception as varying from reception to deception. When we are receptive of our actual needs, we are closer to balance. When we are not, we are dwelling in deception. And illusion.

Always the problem of choosing is the problem of balance; always it is genuine when it is effortless. When desire and intention are in alignment to the self, choosing does not feel like choosing, but like desire expressed and actualized. It is a paradox. Where there is conflict, no genuine choice is being made, for there will be pros and cons left unresolved. We are only moving closer or further away from alignment, dancing around the middle in rhythms of supposing. To choose is to know; to know is to be free of conflict and, thus, if only for the flicker of an eyelash, to be free of the ego.

When we are too drowsy with the consensus trance to choose, the higher (or deeper) levels of the self choose for us. There are no accidents, only learning—as Gary Zukav puts it—through joy or through pain.[7]

In the next chapter, now that we have a map to guide us, we will turn our attention to the problems involved in choosing the self over the ego. That is an immense challenge, but it is the key to framing effective core-need strategies. It is the difference between learning through joy and being taught through pain.

INTERMEZZO

The ego is a perception collector that runs on guilt. Since love is the fundamental energy of the cosmos, guilt is aborted love energy. The ego's main rule is this: Whatever you do to become worthy of love will never be quite enough.

Your ego and mine are not as personal as we think. Since the ego has no inherent content, it must be filled with the fetid, garish contents of the collective ego. Social worlds are egos complete with asphalt and stoplights. They are industrious consensus machines that run on fear. They produce the carnival trinkets, lies, and evasions that are faithlessly recounted in newspapers.

The natural self is spontaneous; it dwells in the many-chambered mansion of now. The ego is a clock.

The natural self is curious. The ego is a box of facts that everyone knows.

The natural self is playful. The ego is a hive drone.

The natural self is sensual. The ego is a sinner, full of sin.

The natural self resonates to beauty and finds it every-where. The ego puts art in museums and certifies who is an artist and who is not.

The heart of the self-in-time is this natural self, this magical child. We are taught that its innocence is naïveté and weakness. In fact, our innocence is both our power and the crucible of our transformation. It is the sacred penta-gram by which we may recognize each other in this strange place that is not our home.

5

Brenden Matrix Geometry: The Quest for What We Really Want

In this world there are only two tragedies. One is not getting what one wants, and the other is getting it.

Oscar Wilde

When we compare the components of the self and of the ego suggested by the Brenden Matrix, we get some insight into how the ego hides our self from us.

Figure 1 is a simpler version of Figure 5 in the preceding chapter, just to keep the imagery in mind. You might want to study the figure a moment to think again about the geometry of the relationships between the ego and the self.

FIGURE 1: THE OPPOSED FACES OF THE EGO AND OF THE SELF

The Ego

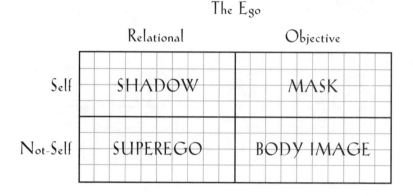

	Relational	Objective
Self	SHADOW	MASK
Not-Self	SUPEREGO	BODY IMAGE

The Self

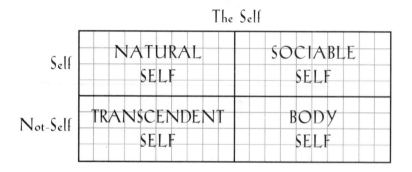

	Relational	Objective
Self	NATURAL SELF	SOCIABLE SELF
Not-Self	TRANSCENDENT SELF	BODY SELF

As you will recall, the shadow obscures the innocence of the natural self, compromising the core need associated with it—the need to give and receive love. The mask hides the playfulness of our sociable self, compromising our core need for social identity and approval. The body image replaces a genuine awareness of our body, too often making our efforts to meet our body needs inappropriate. Worst of all, perhaps, the superego shrouds our awareness of the transcendent self and cuts us off from the source of our identity. It defeats our deep need for cosmic grounding.

By seeing these relationships we may begin to get some ideas about how to deal with them.

LOWERING OUR MASKS TO REVEAL OUR
SOCIABLE SELVES

Our social masks are stiff, humorless shields, held up to hide our natural, sociable playfulness—our sociable self. Therefore, our core need for social identity, associated with this quadrant of the Brenden Matrix, is generally negotiated with counterfeit tender. We present ourselves *as we are not* in order to be acceptable to others, which is a great way to experience more or less continual tension and anxiety. Trying to get recognition for who we are not is a poor core-need strategy.

Of course, because our social world demands sham and pretense, we sometimes have to make false presentations to get along. We may have to play "enthusiastic attentive coworkers" to keep our jobs, for example, or we may have to offer filial affection to relatives we don't like very much. That's not necessarily a bad idea. Even if we know our jobs aren't very fulfilling or feel in our hearts that Uncle Frank is a boring bigot, it makes sense to "put the best face" on whatever social role we find ourselves playing. Attacking ineffective core-need strategies in another won't improve your own. If you can't offer your life energy in fountains of light, it's all right to offer it by the teaspoon.

But we can also begin to recognize what we are doing. And we can begin to find more ways to be our natural, playful, sociable self—to lower our masks. Often, for example, "lightening up" in our social roles, learning to wear them lightly, will be appreciated by others, even if they cannot manage to return the favor.

Now, it would be an error to understand our social masks in purely negative terms. The matter is not quite so simple. While we deplore the need for masks, they may be kinder than the jealousy, the fury, the spite that they cover. Indeed, our masks may sometimes be an effort to present something ideal in us that is not fully present in our sense of self. Masks fashioned for ceremonial dances or even for dramatic purposes may, in fact, allow us to express our deeper selves. The Hopi kachina dancer may, somehow, touch the power of the spirit entity he or she represents. In that way, through a mythology, the people reach out to the dimensions of the self beyond the ego, returning them to the consciousness of the tribe through the patterns of a ceremonial.

On the other hand, a person may also produce a social persona that becomes a "mask of power," one that serves to "reveal by concealing." Charismatic leaders like a Mahatma Gandhi or even an Adolf Hitler managed that, although the differences between their masks were very great.

Gandhi's "mask" of self-effacement and natural simplicity was designed, perhaps self-consciously, to reveal the power of his transcendent self. The Mahatma was about joining the objective and relational domains of his nature. He was honoring the fact that the sociable self and the transcendent self are poles of a single line of force in our lives. Put another way, his social-identity and cosmic-grounding needs were joined, just as thinking and intuition must speak together if we would have wisdom. His persona linked the objective social self to the cosmic domain of the not-self, to his transcendent nature.

Hitler's core-need geometry was quite different from that of Gandhi. When the transcendent self in us is shrouded by guilt, by the superego—which is nearly always the case—we generally try to discharge or project it away from us by finding fault and projecting blame. Or we may assemble our defenses against "unworthiness" around strategies of power and control. This generally amounts to overidentifying with the prestige and privilege of social position. Becoming a lawyer, a physician, a vice president for sales may hide an agenda by which we compensate for the "debt" to our superego. In Hitler's case, I suspect, the scarring of his childhood required a great deal of compensation. He did a quick tour of Nietzsche's *Ubermensch* notion, dipped a toe in the worst of Hegel—his quasi-deification of the state—and decided his Kampf (his "ordeal") deserved a big symbolic S for

"Superman" on his chest. He inverted a sacred symbol—the swastika, which was a sort of mandala symbol to peoples like the Kiowa and the Cherokee—to his purposes, and ascended to the dark strategy of declaring himself "transcendent" of shame and guilt—a "superman." Such dark strategies seem to draw on the power of the shadow directly, because there is no doubt of Hitler's charismatic gifts. But they served fear and intimidation, not ordering for the common good. The ultimate price of that bargain is to become the servant of death—and so he was.

When we cannot get love through relationships that extend and connect our identity to the cosmos, we will generally try to get the love energy we need through unleashing the terrorist potential of the shadow. If we cannot feed on love, we will feed on its counterfeit, on fear disguised as love. That can seem to work because, where there are tyrants, there will always be sycophants. There will be people who shun their natural self in favor of being "good children" who must obey the "stern father." Eric Hoffer called them "true believers."[1] Faulty core-need strategies complement each other.

Of course, a Hitler could not rise to power in a world of self-awareness. On the other hand, in such a world, perhaps, a Gandhi would not be necessary.

In any case, the key to managing the mask aspect of our ego lies in the playfulness of our natural self. We can learn to pay attention to what we are doing when we play social roles, to avoid overidentifying with them, to wear them lightly. Also, to the extent that we are able to recognize our social roles as games required by a particular social game board, we gain some control over the moves we make and the game pieces we choose.

LOOSENING THE CHAINS OF THE BODY IMAGE

In Western social worlds, certainly in the United States, there is a huge, inappropriate emphasis on body appearance. We are all encouraged to be anxious about how our bodies look to others. Advertising and media generally bombard us with messages about our bodily flaws. Sometimes these messages are direct. Advertisers quite deliberately attempt to create "markets" by creating "needs." We are asked to feel bad about our hairlines, our thighs, our bellies, our less-than-odorless bodies, then offered the remedy. For a price. Other media messages are less direct, though not necessarily subtle. The models for the covers of women's magazines are typically cultural ideals of feminine beauty, frequently offering us mammary landscapes that defy the laws of physics. Television programming tends to emphasize youth and physical beauty so persistently that I sometimes wonder if Americans—who typically watch television several hours a day—may tend to forget what ordinary people look like. Or perhaps they assume that there are two worlds: Celebrity-Land, where the beautiful people live, and Gray-World, where less-than-real people sit in offices or stare vacantly from the windows of buses.

As an artist I have spent many hours drawing live nude models, male and female. Out of that experience, I have wondered if, in a saner world, it would be helpful if there were various social settings where ordinary people, men and women, could be nude together. The actuality of real bodies might alert us to the uniqueness of actual physical appearances. We might learn to see the beauty in different kinds of body types at different ages. We might also learn a level of body acceptance that would help us see our bodies and those of others with less judgment. The centerfold and the muscular underwear model might fall into a healthier perspective.

In any case, even without advertisers to aggravate the situation, the ego, by its nature, wants us to identify with our physical bodies—to see ourselves as separated objects in our own little worlds. We are encouraged to carry around an anxious sensitivity to how our bodies appear to others, since only in the meetings of bodies do our little worlds ever seem to touch. That sensitivity gives rise to the ego's body image. Just as the body in proper perspective is a vehicle for expression, for giving and receiving the energy of the natural self in all its forms, the body image is an illusory vehicle that speaks the language of the shadow.

The body image is experienced as an image or sense of how we imagine we look to others. It is decidedly not the same thing as being in touch with our actual bodies. It is a vague, inner image, a projection. Partly, it is persistent, like a bad habit. It is almost always inaccurate. Thin women may be convinced that they are "fat." Men of average height may be vaguely certain they are a bit taller—unless that bit of projection is challenged. Then they may wonder why they suddenly feel threatened or depressed. We tend to nag at ourselves about certain body features we imagine to be less than ideal. Our breasts are too small or too large; our penises are too small (almost never too large); our tummies not flat enough—and so on.

While that "not-ideal" part of the body image is pretty persistent, we also tend continually to modify our inner "body-image approval rating" when we interact with others. Consciously or unconsciously, we look for hints or clues in the mirror of others' real or imagined consciousness of our appearance. We try to see "who we are" in the eyes of others, and awareness of our imagined body appearance is a part of that imaginary self. Our ego self. We would like reassurance that we are tall enough, that we don't have fat thighs, that our receding hairline makes us look "intellectual," not "old." But, in general, no amount of reassurance will last as long as a particular body image persists.

Evaluating others' real or imagined judgments of us is, of course, one of the ways the ego takes on its particular form in each of us. It is a process that involves more than our body image. Every aspect of the ego is built through the imagined judgments of others. Sociologist Charles Horton Cooley called this constructed identity in us the "looking-glass self." We learn to imagine who we are by imagining others' judgments of us. We are, therefore, liable to multiply our self-delusions by two. Another's partial vision of who we are, multiplied by our judgments of our imagined sense of their judgments, is a lovely little recipe for pain, confusion, and an absolute minimum of intimacy in our relationships with others.

In any case, the elemental core-need strategy for getting through the body image to the body—and its actual needs for reasonable attention to grooming, some food, some shelter, and some exercise—is body awareness. Body awareness can be practiced by paying attention to our actual body sensations, to the actual experience of being in a body through objective or inner presence. The objective of that work is to accept the body as it is, without judgment. But there may be informative side effects to such inquiries.

We may recognize that our physical body is not, actually, "who we are." Perhaps that should not surprise us too much. Scientific evidence shows us that our physical body is anything but constant. It is rather like what we might see from a distance if swarms of tiny moths danced around a light source that had the shape of a human body. We replace cells, molecules, and atoms at a remarkable rate. Every morning we wake up with a different body. Still, that fact can be a strange discovery, particularly in a culture like ours. It leads us toward a different feeling about the nature of our reality.

One of the first times I discovered this object, property of my body, I was sitting in a bathtub. I was about fifteen. Looking at my hand, I realized that it was not "me," but part of a "thing" I "used" somehow. I was certainly in a body—one in the hormonal storms of adolescence—but, somehow, I also knew that I was not my body. Later on, pushed by the consensus trance, I would doubt this sort of direct experience, reading that such a sense of detachment might be characteristic of a psychotic state. So, as most of us would, I "revised" my interpretation of such experiences, and, for a long time, simply lived in my body image without questioning it much. But that is an error. What we experience in quietness is what we experience. To discover the self, we must honor what we learn from it.

The second discovery one makes about the actual body, and, for me, a gradual, ongoing process, is that it is, in some way, the face of an energy "field." That field is intimately associated with the mind. To discover this, try an exercise. Move your finger. Be present and nonjudgmental about how you do this. An American psychic and artist, Ingo Swann, spent many hours in scientific laboratories having his abilities to leave his body and perform other "impossible tricks" measured and analyzed. He was once asked to demonstrate psychokinesis. He lifted his finger and wriggled it. "Do you believe it?" he asked.[2]

The issue is not mind over matter. To paraphrase Sir James Jeans, commenting on what quantum physics had done to materialism, matter is mind stuff. The relationship between your awareness and your body is dependent on your consciousness state. In some such states you can walk on hot coals, in others you can fly, in still others you get acid indigestion.

Today, of course, as we discover the limitations of conventional Western, medicine, older, traditional forms of therapy that recognize this "second" or energy body are becoming more familiar to us. Chinese herbal medicine, acupuncture, chakra meditations and body work, Ayurvedic medicine, the system behind martial arts—from Tai Chi to Kung Fu—are "technologies" with varying models of understanding about this second body. Exploring them can help you experience directly what you are beyond your physical body.

While discovering that we—like all living creatures—have "energy-information fields" that organize the atoms, molecules, and cells of our body is certainly useful, and while the energy body may be closer to who we are than the physical body, that is not our identity either. Ultimately, what we are is not confined in space-time and is not, by ordinary definitions "local," except as we identify with our "location."

On being asked if humans have souls, a character in one of my plays responds:

"No, not really."
"Ha! Just as I thought!"
"The question is misleading."
"Misleading?"
"Souls have humans beings."

What we are contains who we imagine we are, and that includes the body. But we are more than physical bodies. If we were not, you could not move your finger to turn this page.

LOOKING INTO THE SHADOW

We have within us powers of creation and of destruction, of ordering and chaos. We can "invert" our need for love into a need to gain power over others, to destroy—which is the same thing. Tyrants have always been warlords of various kinds, because the ultimate god of power over others is death.

Until the world is mended, there is a proper role for the warrior in us. But that role is not to gain power over others; it is to overcome fear in ourselves and in others. Fear is what we experience when we are not conscious of love's presence, of the life energy that is the pulsating rhythm of Being. The power of the shadow side of our nature includes the power of the warrior and calls on the virtues of patience, courage, and boldness. But the warrior is only necessary because we have made social worlds that have split us into two parts—an imagined ego and a dimly remembered self—which, like the two ways of knowing, seem beyond reconciliation.

You will recall from the preceding chapter that the natural self in each of us has five dimensions. Our magical child is curious, spontaneous, playful, sensual, and sensitive to beauty. Our life energy, Eros, suffuses all of these dimensions.

The shadow is the dark side of every face of the natural self. It is the use of our life energy to attract the love we need when we think neither we nor others really deserve it. It is the substitution of fear—which is the meaning of our efforts to gain power over others—for love.

CURIOSITY BECOMES DETACHMENT

When our natural curiosity allows us to expose animals to lethal doses of radiation—just to measure the results—we are operating out of the dark side of our nature, alone or together. And the agenda of such horrors, always, is the illusion that we gain power by controlling others—or by controlling the natural world. Curiosity, in this dark guise, acts not so much to reveal as to reduce what is present to its imagined elements, to dissociate the whole into its parts, and to separate our selves from that which we objectify. The dark side of modern science, of course, resides in this cold objectivism.

Curiosity separated from our sense of beauty, from our playfulness, from our spontaneity, from our sensuality is dangerous. It makes us learn that what we are curious about has nothing much to do with us. When our minds explore the world and conclude that we are separate and alone, we have entered the domain of the ego's greatest power over us and touched the ashes of our most persistent delusion. As long as we are rooted in that illusion we will imagine that our thoughts and actions are only our own and, thus, ultimately, that they have no meaning. Out of that sort of consciousness, curiosity, joined to the quest for power, becomes unspeakable cruelty. The Nazi "scientists" who immersed frightened, hopeless people in freezing water to measure their reactions demonstrate that sort of consciousness.

Auschwitz, Dachau, Treblinka are monuments to the ego struggling to define itself in darkness, to take revenge on remorseless time, to honor the archetype of blood-red Mars and its attendants—fear and death.

WE BECOME HARDENED TO THE RAPE OF HARMONY

When our natural sensitivity to beauty is cast into our shadow nature, it reemerges as parodies of beauty. Our shadow nature is, roughly, how we act when we allow our natural self to remain veiled by denying and repressing our desire nature. In this way, of course, we allow ourselves to associate guilt and shame with spontaneous and natural expressions of our life energy. Our propensities to intertwine the garish and the natural is the strange result. We learn to choose Las Vegas neon and become indifferent to a desert sunset; we sense, perhaps, but cannot tell the difference between the dance of sunlight on a mountain stream and the muted rainbow of a gasoline-polluted puddle on a field of asphalt. We learn to ignore the stark brutality of abandoned apartment buildings, their shattered windows like the eyes of corpses. We accept the eerie ugliness of a slag heap in what was once a pristine valley. Our conditioned sense of beauty becomes a muted awareness strained through our shadow, through the deepest power of the ego to deny.

The shadow language of beauty is a remarkable and persistent aspect of art. That is because art, if it has value, is about our relational nature, and while we live with duality and with egos, that includes the chaos of the shadow. The power of Edvard Munch's paintings and of the Expressionists generally, of Picasso's *Guernica*, of Goya's depictions of war, are not "pretty." They touch the shadow side of us and make us wince. Modern art is often shadow art, full of shock and gimmicks, because that is the only relational language guilt can approve.

We Try to Control Time

The shadow side of spontaneity in the natural self is the myth of Kronos, the god that eats its children. Now, if you recall from Chapter 2, Chronos (and yes, the difference in spelling is intentional) is the flow of events around us that are always in flux. It is the experiential quality of being in a body in the domain of time-space. Chronos—a Greek word for time—is the name we gave this existential domain. But the experience of time is the experience of limitation and of powerlessness. Time limits are restraints, intractable evidence of our impotence against aging and death. To reckon time, to agonize over how much of it we "waste" or "spend" or "lose," is to feel dwarfed by that which ultimately seems to consume our lives.

Spontaneity, being present in the moment, is both the antithesis of our normal experience of being trapped in a body in time, and its only remedy. As the Christian mystic Meister Eckehart put it, "the greatest enemy of spiritual awareness is our idea of time." The only moment we live in is now. The only moment that can be real for us is now. The only place from which we may choose is now. And now is always present. Your now is present before you entered the body you imagine is your identity, is present as you read these words, is present when you are not in-physical, during sleep, or when you are not engaged in the Earth field. Now is where you are, have been, will be. It is a sacred no-time at the center of supposing.

We Try to Regiment Our Natural Playfulness

The shadow side of playfulness, of our natural sociability, is our dreams of power in search of love. We confuse our power over others with an affirmation of our own power and, therefore, of our value. We imagine that the transient satisfactions of another's obeisance to our rank, our status, our manipulation games can give us the self-approval that, in fact, is only fulfilled in the experience of knowing that we are loved and lovable.

The essence of these fevered dreams is regimentation, which is Kronos's first cousin. Regimentation is the pattern that emerges when we allow hierarchies of ranked statuses—at work, in our families—to become measures of personal worth and value. The organization of sport around agendas of stark competition is about regimenting play for profit. The cadence of a marching regiment stirs our shadow nature and reverberates to nationalism—which, at its heart, is always about power over others. We play at cops and robbers (or at overcoming beasts of prey in computer games) to learn that play is about competing with ourselves or with other players for control. And for self-worth.

Regimentation, ultimately, is an effort to order time, and thus to pretend for a while that we control it. A direct effect of the hierarchically regimented roles in a society is to make the time of the person in the higher status seem more valuable than that of the person of lesser rank. A doctor's time is more "valuable" than a patient's. A company president's time is more "valuable" than a secretary's time. And so on.

Western social worlds are so saturated in time-control agendas that many have suggested that the elemental symbol of our lives is a clock. From the advent of Newtonian science—which imagined the cosmos as a sort of cosmic clock—to the anxious comparison of fractions of a second in the hundred-yard dash, not to know "what time it is" is not to know what's going on. If you aren't with the time-control program, you are considered irrational. Our present generation of children are learning their time-control lessons from video games. The "Mario Brothers" are about providing the skills for potential jet-fighter pilots, and the impatient anxiety to zap the beast before the beast zaps you betrays the sharing that is at the heart of playfulness.

Trying to control time is a side effect of trying to gain control over others in our faulty quest for love. We have all heard the expression "time is money." But what is money if not a dream of power? The cadences of the industrial age, from the monotonous drone of steam looms and the endless nodding of oil-well pumps to the endless parade of diesel trucks, are efforts to control time. They are characterized by monotony, alienation, and the gray mists of fear that are so often translated as cynicism and a bitter sense of irony. Our playfulness, stripped of natural innocence, will try to find humor in all this—like some stand-up comic's shtick on racism, fast food, and freeway shootings. But the comedy is a face of tragedy. Like Charlie Chaplin's character in the film *Modern Times*, we are lost in ruins we cannot interpret and that do not nurture us.

Always in regimentation there is a parody of life. A marching regiment is a parody of a tribal dance—and the differences between them are stark. The regiment marches in the tick-tock of clock time, to archetypal Kronos's martial tempo; the tribal dance moves in sacred time, the nonlinear time of interacting consciousness states that the Greeks called *kairos*. The slightly comic (therefore, playful and joyous) aspect of a marching Dixieland band is the odd blending of nonregimented *kairos* time, tribal and relational in nature, with the regimented tempos idealized in Western music.

Do not misunderstand. The quest for beauty in the harmonies of number, order, and symmetry is not evil. Bach is beautiful in part because his tempos are so symmetrical and precise. But the tempo is not where the beauty lies. It lies in the complementarity of chaos and order, of the relational and the objective. Compare the increments of tempo in "Jesu, Joy of Man's Desiring," for example, with the accents of the melody—which are rich and unpredictable, a "chaos pattern" like a human heartbeat. Bach blends the relational and the objective, order and organic "chaos," thus becoming timeless.

The problem of regimentation is one of imbalance, of entrancement. Industrial, regimented rhythms—whether of monotonously turning cam shafts or the cadenced crunch of jackboots—are like the steady click-clack of a windshield wiper on a long drive. We slip into a trance. We forget what we are doing.

What we mainly forget is that our natural sociability is about playing together, not about competing with each other for love and attention. For, clearly, the shadow side of playfulness is found in our social games, our shadow games.

We still play games in our social masks, but they are cruel. We play at being the center of attention, at being "the prettiest" or "the best." The games have hidden or not-so-hidden agendas. And the agendas are very often about gaining an advantage, imposing one's own ego over another's, having the last word, "being right," having one's own point of view accepted and another's defeated. Learning that bitter lesson is a necessary dis-illusion in the quest for self-knowledge.

Our power struggles with others are faulty core-need strate-gies in search of self-acceptance on the one hand, and taking power away from anyone who will let us as a substitute for get-ting the love we need on the other. We can find better ways to get what we want.

SENSUALITY BECOMES SIN

Certainly one of the strangest effects of Western social worlds on our natural self is the wholesale transport of all things sensual into the barbed-wire enclosure of guilt. Part of the problem, I suppose, is our obsession with orgasms as the apogee of sensual pleasure. Not that I would wish to deny the charm of orgasms; I only question the context into which their meaning has been cast. I suppose, as someone said, there is not really any such thing as a "bad orgasm." If the issue were chocolate—for one who adores chocolate—we might rate Godiva over Nestlés but take pleasure from whichever was available. On the other hand, if we associate the best of sensual pleasure with sin—and Western culture has been persistently devoted to that tedious work—surely lesser sensual pleasures may become tainted. And they have. In American society, certainly, asceticism and the work ethic fit together far more like a horse and carriage than do love and marriage.

Not that I am an apostle of hedonism—whatever that may mean since the flower children got jobs as investment bankers and moved to the suburbs. Joy and the fulfillment of our desire nature *is* the goal, but sensualism, hedonism, is not the correct route. Hedonism is tantamount to rebellion and the rejection of social order. Sometimes, as during the sixties, that may be a useful and creative response to a social order that seems monotonously death-oriented. For a while. But sensuality is not sensualism, not a serviceable ism of any sort. Sensuality is a channel for expressing the natural self, not an end in itself.

While rejection of the body and of the sensual is a relational-mode error, an attempt to "be good" by being unreal, addictions to sensation as an end in itself—the compulsive pursuit of pleasurable sensation—is an objective-mode error. We ascribe more to the objective realm than it can deliver. Recall that the realm of conditioned perception is the primary domain of illusion.

Sensuality, on the other hand, is a natural inheritance. In Wim Wenders's wonderful film *Wings of Desire,* angels hover around humans doing their gentle work, yet sometimes long for sensual experience. In the film, Peter Falk—playing the part of an angel who has slipped across the space-time boundary for a vacation "in-physical"—speaks to an angel who's thinking about doing the same. Like a cryptic Walt Whitman, he tells a companion angel about the weight and warmth of a coffee mug, the smell of the coffee, the bite of cold air, the taste of tobacco smoke. Being sensual is being aware of the crisp boundary between being in a body and experiencing what that is like. To be sensual is not unlike practicing objective presence; it is paying attention.

Sensuality can certainly be about having and giving pleasure, but all that we imagine about that, from hugs and kisses to body massages, to wild and woolly bedroom gymnastics, are only part of a spectrum. Some colors of that spectrum are often thought sinful, some pleasurable—especially if they should be sinful—while some of the spectrum of sensuality is thought of as painful. Raindrops on your head can simply be experienced and enjoyed or found irritating and annoying. Shoveling snow can be a challenging game or an agony. Meanwhile, other parts of the spectrum of things sensual are merely ignored. How many Americans pay attention to the taste of their food? The sound of rain? The quality of light on another's face?

Having touched on the matter of pain, I should like to make a comment. Namely, I do not think pain is a necessary burden of sensuality, of living in a body in time. God knows there is pain here, in cancer wards and kitchens, in bedrooms and on playgrounds. Everywhere. But I have come to suspect that much of that pain is a product of our collective entrancements, and is not inevitable. A large portion of what we experience as pain is fear, after all. The fact that simple self-hypnosis techniques can alleviate the discomforts of many sorts of dental and medical procedures supports that thesis. For what happens in hypnosis is a subtle shift out of ordinary waking consciousness into a "side state" that is closer to the observer aspect of consciousness and a bit distanced from the actor. That permits us to experience some control over our experience, which allows a reduction of fear. Moving from habitual ego awareness to self-awareness can reduce fear even more.

As more and more of us take the quiet journey to the self, changing the nature of our collective consciousness, I dream and trust that our pain will be less. Then, at last, among the magical children of Earth, sensuality may yet be, simply, what it is, remarkable, mysterious, and—fun.

THE NOT-SO-SUPEREGO

To make guilty is to undermine another's cosmic grounding, to push him or her away from the center. To make oneself guilty is to turn away from one's transcendent self and to pretend that one has no center. Making guilty is a power stratagem. Therefore, it is a faulty core-need strategy for getting love by feeding on fear—which, in the case of parents' dominating their children, may then be called "love." Accepting guilt is a faulty core-need strategy for getting identity and approval in one's social world. Where egos interact, the two faulty strategies complement each other. Making guilty and accepting guilt are a persistent pattern between parents and children, married couples, friends, bosses and subordinates. It is an elemental process in the destruction of innocence and the creation of the veil behind which we hide from love. It is a pattern that poisons our experience of each other and the world.

The currency of the superego is guilt. The effect of guilt is to make us feel unworthy. Being convinced that we are unworthy renders us unable to accept the radiant power of our natural self and, thus, blind to the spiritual dimensions at the foundation of our life and our consciousness.

When, at the level of social institutions, organized religion takes on the properties of the superego, it has the same poisonous effect. It teaches us we have no center, that our center is elsewhere—in a sermon, in a chalice, in a book. By teaching us we have no center, superego religion instructs us in the ghostly arts of guilt and sin, and the wages of guilt and sin is fear. Love, which is the only real power we have, does not spring from fear.

Religion that is about innocence and freedom from guilt and, thus, freedom from the need to attack others, to gain power over them, is a religion of love. The first sort of religion is about the ego, the second about the nature and power of the self. That we live in a world where both of these social creatures are called by the same word is a symptom of our collective dis-ease.

The only loving purpose religion can have is the revelation of the self to the self. Among its tasks must be the re-visioning of our social worlds, the discovery of our entrancement, so that we may awaken together. In fact, as far as I can tell, that is part of what Jesus taught. He rebuked the entrenched priesthood, paid loving attention to socially unacceptable women, and hung out with Matthew, an enforcer for the Roman syndicate. He healed on the Sabbath, violating the laws of the Hebrew social world in honor of principles that do not participate in the fevered dreaming of such worlds.

By tearing away the veils of illusion concealed as social tradition and custom, we expose the alarming fact that a social world is very much like a collective ego. It has the same dynamics and the same kinds of goals. That is a hard lesson. What's in the newspapers and on television, in our song lyrics and shopping malls, in our paychecks and our life-insurance policies, in our courtrooms, and schoolrooms, and bathrooms, in our prepackaged conceptions and processed foods, is the ectoplasm of entrancement. We have made a world that does not know us, that does not nurture us.

Before we emerge into self-knowledge, into light, the quest for the self must take us across a dark valley of dis-illusion. Beyond dis-illusion, in stillness, we discover the pain built into our projections, our delusions. We find that the meaning of the self is found in our relationships, and that the relational order of the cosmos is about love and healing that are natural to us. The ego is a fortress for isolating us; the self is the narrow gate into that infinite field in which all of us are connected.

INTERMEZZO

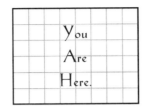

Paradox is transformed in an alchemy.
The alchemy is a transmutation,
a separating of wheat from tares,
of the self from the ego's serpent coils,
of gold from base metal.

The metamorphosis of consciousness
springs from
no dance of molecules,
no energetic attack on quarks,
no righteous wrestling with quirks,
but from an ancient vision
that is deep enough
and high enough
to free us from the shadows
of time's intemperate dance.

6

Our Core-Need Geometry: Still Looking for What We Really Want

Down-hearted doubters, dull and excluded,
Frivolous sullen moping angry affected
disheartened atheistical,
I know every one of you,
and know the unspoken interrogatories,
By experience I know them.

Walt Whitman

Nothing can block love's power except our will not to accept it. Yet, since life-love-energy is the only energy there is, the will to reject love must come from a misuse of love energy. It does. Guilt is the misuse of love energy. It is an effort to "hold" life energy in abeyance until we feel we "deserve" it. Since the guilt load is not, actually, natural to the self, we try various ways to off-load it, to discharge it from the psychic system. Most of the time we try to do that through compensation, through the endless apology for ourselves we present to the world through the mask aspect of the ego. We compensate by exchanging innocence and our natural power for tokens of self-esteem—social status, more money, a bigger house in a better neighborhood. Not that there is anything inherently wrong about feeling at home in one's social world, using money as a medium of exchange, or living in a pleasant and graceful environment. If we did not see these things out of the consciousness of scarcity egonomics, they would be harmless and useful. But that is not the case. Our drive for money and status is too often informed by fear, not love, by self-rejection, not self-extension.

The underlying experience of identifying with the ego (which is self-rejection) is fear. And fear, ultimately, is the experience of being alone with guilt. If we cannot get rid of stored guilt energy through the compensation-for-guilt afforded us by approved social roles, the guilt energy becomes anger, rage. When rage and anger leave a persistent sediment in our awareness, the result is hatred. In any case, where there is anger, rage, or hatred, we are struggling to regain life energy we think we have lost. The part of us that knows we are deserving of love, imagining it has been cut off from love's power, rebels.

Sudden anger is a discharge of guilt energy when compensating strategies (thought strategies that make us feel reasonably secure and okay about ourselves) fail temporarily. For example, you find Becky's bike in the driveway when you are about to back the car out of the garage. Unfortunately, you are already primed for rage by having allowed yourself to feel threatened; knowing it would make you mad, you just read a newspaper editorial supporting the destruction of fragile wetlands. Becky skips out of the house, blithely ignoring her bike, headed for the school bus.

Kaboom. Becky learns a quick, sharp-tongued lesson about bicycles in driveways and her father's inexplicable rage.

Of course, most of us will then attack ourselves for "losing our temper," for losing control of the balance-of-fear strategies approved by the ego ideal. The ego ideal is fragile. It is a projection, a sort of inner program, that tells us how we are supposed to act and feel; it attempts to "fit" our sense of self-worth to some set of social norms with which we identify. You can get a pretty good idea of what your own ego ideal is like by making a list of all the "shoulds" and "should-nots" you feel apply to "good people." Since the ego ideal is not rooted in the self, but in the ego, it has weak grounding. It tells us how we're supposed to act and feel, but it is not connected to the power of the natural self. Awareness rooted in the self guides our feelings and actions with effortless grace. Awareness rooted in the ego is defensive and uncertain. It leaves us vulnerable to anger.

Hatred—the toxic sediment of anger and rage—is the experience of fear as a void of cruel powerlessness. Hatred and its endless expressions, from bigotry to rape, becomes dominant in our ego strategies when we decide we cannot have the power we need to survive any other way. There is not, perhaps, any real expectation of getting the love we long for through hatred and violence, but there is a desire to destroy life energy, to destroy love itself. In metaphysical terms, attack out of hatred is an effort to destroy God, to destroy our Source. It is, therefore, insane by any conceivable definition. In any case, in the individual, when hatred is expressed as direct attack, as violence, it is always out of a failure of scarcity egonomics to get us what we want, or, at least, what we think we want.

When hatred is expressed as collective will in social worlds, as in America's insane "war on drugs" or in our social policies that would end crime by building ever more prisons and brutalizing ever more people for ever longer periods of time, there are imbalances in that social world. The imbalances produce a shared disease, which allows people to be enlisted to the ranks of those who would destroy love. For there is a tacit consensus in these situations, always denied and rationalized, that death is more real than life, that fear is stronger than love.

Now we will attempt to understand where guilt comes from and to see how ego geometry is an inversion or distortion of the potential of the self.

FUNCTION PATHS

Our psychic functions, our core needs and, therefore, the aspects of our ego and of our self, are linked by what we will call "function paths." A function *path* is a direct connection between psychic functions, like thinking and intuition. It is a *function* path because the functions work together. You can't have effective thinking without intuition; you can't have useful intuitions unless you can think about them. Understanding how the function paths connect our core needs helps us see what we are doing that is, literally, self-defeating. Actually, as you will see, we have already been talking about function paths—when we were comparing Hitler and Gandhi in the last chapter, for example—but we didn't use that name. Now we will.

Function paths have roughly the same nature in any matrix set—whether it is about the ego, the self, a social group, or a whole culture. To help us relate them to actual experience, we'll look first at how these paths work in social worlds. We'll do that for two reasons. First, all of us need to get used to the idea that personal and collective worlds are not really separable. Contrary to popular opinion, we do not live all alone in the cage of our skulls; we just think we do. Your life world and mine are connected in the web of our social-consensus reality. When that consensus reality does not allow us to be aware of our core needs or pursue effective core-need strategies, we share hell. On the other hand, even if your ego and mine cannot speak the same language, your self and mine live together, in a harmonic resonance beyond space time. Each of us is part of the transcendent design that is our home. We share heaven.

Second, this is not simply a digression in sociological theory. We are going to get at something that needs to be understood if we are to move toward self-awareness, namely, the nature of social roles. For, whether you realize it or not, we express our ego ideal or our self-awareness by playing roles that only have meaning in our particular social world.

Looking at Figure 1, you will see that the function paths can be thought of as diagonal or vertical lines connecting the four-fold structure of the self (or the ego, or the core needs) or, for that matter, the terms assigned to any matrix set.

FIGURE 1: THE FUNCTION PATHS FOR ANY MATRIX SET

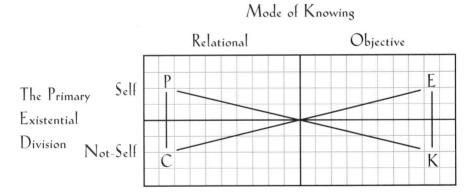

The letters P, E, K, and C are meant to recall the four existential realms of our experience discussed in Chapter 2: psyche, ethos, chronos, and cosmos. But they may also simply be thought of as place holders, like mathematical notations. Why? Because some *aspect* of each existential domain is represented in *any* matrix set. It doesn't matter if the matrix set nests Jung's psychic

functions, our core needs, or Fiske's four modes of social relations; any such fourfold set tells us something about how we
experience the fourfold dimensions of our existence.

The diagonal path C–E represents the function path that
links thinking and intuition in our consciousness. It also represents a direct link between our core need for social identity (feeling we have a place in our social world) and our core need for
cosmic grounding. Since the C and E quadrants are always related
to finding our place in the world, the function path between
them—in any matrix set—is called the "ordering axis."

The diagonal path P–K represents the function path that links
Jung's feeling and sensation functions. Therefore, it also links our
need for giving and receiving love to our need for body maintenance and survival. Since the love-life-energy-body expression
dimensions of our consciousness are about expressing who we are,
through working, playing, loving, it is called the "expression axis."

The vertical line P–C represents the nature of the connection
between our feeling and intuition functions. It also represents
the way our need for giving and receiving love is related to our
need for cosmic grounding. Now, all of the psychic functions and
all of our core needs work together as a single system. But the
links between the pairs of psychic functions or pairs of core needs
are distinctive. Feeling (associated with the P quadrant) and
intuition (in the C quadrant) are not related to each other in the
same way as feeling and sensation (associated with the P and K
quadrants). The "path" has a different quality. Your feeling states,
for example, are immediately correlated to the biochemicals in
your bloodstream. Happy feelings make endorphins; angry feelings make adrenaline. Or, less efficiently, epinephrine, adminis-
tered as a drug, eventually makes happy feelings, and so on. In
fact, you can alter your feeling state very quickly by altering your
body state—by simply breathing more evenly, for example. On
the other hand, your feeling state *mirrors* your cosmic-grounding
state. Feeling at home and safe in the universe is quite different

from feeling that the universe is hostile or indifferent. That is, the repertoire of feelings available to you is qualitatively different. For one thing, in the first condition, mirroring a sense of place and safety in the cosmos, you can be generous and loving. You are spiritually wealthy. In the second condition, you can hardly afford to be civil, much less loving. You are spiritually impoverished. In any case, because feelings mirror your intuitive insights into what is real and because your capacity to give and receive love mirrors the state of your cosmic grounding, we call the P–C connection a mirror path. Specifically, the P–C link is the *relational mirror path* in any matrix set.

The vertical line E–K in any matrix set, is the *objective mirror path*. For example, our sensation and thinking functions have a sort of "looking glass" relationship. We think of a sunny sky as a simile for happy thoughts, of a cloudy sky as a simile for sad thoughts. In effect, our thoughts tend to mirror our body's sense perceptions (including internal pleasure or pain states) and vice versa. Similarly, our sense of our social identity tends to mirror our state of body security (having our body needs met). In a similar way, for a different sort of matrix set, the way a society's economy is set up (K quadrant) tends strongly to mirror the arrangements of social roles (E quadrant) and the way they are ranked. Or vice versa.

You may be wondering why there are not function paths between P and E (feeling and thinking, for example) or C and K (cosmic grounding and the body needs, for example). The four quadrants all represent domains of a single consciousness field or system, after all, so they must be related. True. But these relationships tend to be antagonistic. For example, our core need to give and receive love is often in conflict with our need for social identity and approval, just as our core need for body survival seems at odds with spiritual principles. Jesus' reminder that we do not "live by bread alone," may seem utterly paradoxical when we are afraid of losing our jobs.

In general, the immediate link between opposed quadrants across the relational-objective boundary appears to be indirect. For example, the relationship between your thoughts and your emotional or feeling states may be mediated by your body state. That's why a meditative state that calms the body can settle or moderate both one's feelings and one's thoughts. Similarly, your feeling and thinking states may also be mediated through your intuition states. In terms of core needs, this means that your love needs and your social-identity needs may be brought into closer harmony as your sense of place and security in the cosmos is enhanced.

In a society, as you will see in the illustrations we'll give below, the antagonisms between our core needs reflect imbalances built into the social order.

How Function Paths Work in a Society

To get a feel for how these paths work, remember that they are mainly about the way our four core needs work together in different areas of our lives. For example, there are four primary social institutions—family or community, economy, religion, and some sort of socially endorsed power structure. In modern societies the characteristic power structure is the state; in tribal cultures it might be an informal circle of elders.

The tendency of all societies in all cultures to develop these primary institutions reflects what Talcott Parsons called the "functional requisites" of a society. The "requisites" (things required) are "functional" (have functions) because people in any society have the same four core needs. The primary institutions arise because human behavior derives from trying to meet these needs—consciously or unconsciously.

In Figure 2, we see how the primary institutions look in a matrix set. Notice by reference to Figure 1 that state and religion are on the ordering axis. Family and economy are on the expression axis. When power and religion are institutionalized—and to the extent that those institutions have formal roles and established norms (laws or dogmas, for example)—they order and structure a society. On the expression axis, communal groups that include family and kinship arrangements of some kind are closely related to the nature of the economy or mode of production.

FIGURE 2: FOUR PRIMARY SOCIAL INSTITUTIONS IN A MATRIX SET

	Relational	Objective
Self	Communal Group (Family)	Power Hierarchy (The State)
Not-Self	Legitimating Complex (Religion)	Mode of Production (Economy)

Let's use the example of a tribal culture, the Hopi of Arizona, to see how the function paths of these primary social institutions work together.

As in many tribal cultures, the dominant mentality of the Hopi emphasizes relational-mode knowing, and the mode of production (the way the people make a living) is based primarily on horticulture, in particular, growing corn. Putting aside the complications produced by being a relational culture surrounded by a Western, objective-mode culture, the kinship structure and community arrangements of the Hopi tend to reflect the way the people make a living. The cycle of corn cultivation through the seasons shapes the patterns of community life.

But the patterns of that community life also "mirror" what we call "religion" (on the P—C mirror path). That is, community and religious ideas tend to reflect each other. Emile Durkheim even produced a theory of religion as a sort of "cosmic projection" of the collective consciousness of a community—heaven as a sort of divine village. Of course, in relational cultures like Hopi, there may be no separate word for religion, since ideas about the nature of reality and of the sacred are simply part of everyday life. That is partly because institutions are not as clearly differentiated in tribal cultures and partly because the relational-mode consciousness dominant in such societies sees aspects of life as a system—like that represented in the medicine wheels of the American Plains Indians. The people, the Earth, and the sacred way of being in harmony with life are all parts of a great circle. As cultures evolve into more complex forms, the primary institutions become more clearly differentiated, and lots of other institutional forms emerge, like education, law, sports, the arts, and so on. The new, differentiated institutions tend to emerge out of the primary institutions, however, and will continue to be either expressive or ordering in nature. Education and law are ordering institutions, for example, the first emerging initially from the hegemony over literacy of the priest class of agricultural states, the second emerging as the state evolved solutions to complex problems of order in patriarchal, militaristic states. Organized sports and institutionalized patterns in the arts (symphony orchestra companies, for example) emerged initially out of the expressive activities of people singing or telling stories, or making art together. Art in preliterate cultures, since it is part of community life, mirrors the ordering model of the sacred. Important art in tribal cultures has sacred uses and motifs. In modern cultures, the communal-expressive and the sacred-ordering mirror paths are shattered and the arts may have little to do with community and daily life. But that is another matter, which could take a book all by itself.

The expression axis in Hopi culture consists of the complementarity of communal and economic life. The kinship system reckons sanguineal relationships in the mother's line. You would get your name from your mother, not your father. Because the Hopi social world is organized in matrilineal clans, women traditionally owned houses, for example, and passed them on to their daughters. Married couples were "imbedded" in the clan structure, and divorce, if it occurred, was not so damaging to children, since they remained surrounded by the mother's kin. The male authority figure in cultures like Hopi is not a child's father, but the mother's brother.

Daily life—the business of getting food, preparing it, sharing meals, making pots, cultivating the corn—was the expressive web of making a living, and all of these things were nested in communal life. Their economy was much closer to what the word comes from. Oikos, the root of the word in Greek, means "household." Daily life and all its expressions take place in kinship networks, in "households."

The ordering axis in Hopi is not much like what we are used to. Religion is the ordering pattern mirrored in community life. On the objective side, the perennial problem of "who gets to decide" (the power problem) gave rise in Hopi culture to a consensual manner of making decisions, a process that mirrors the cooperative efforts necessary in their mode of production. When a more rigid power hierarchy was needed to order the efforts of the people, as in time of war, "war chiefs" tended to be appointed on an ad hoc basis—as was true of many American Indian cultures. There was no rationally organized state because there was no need for one.

In any social world the power system consists mainly of the hierarchical ranking of social roles, and these arrangements mirror the mode of production (the E–K mirror path). When tribal cultures evolved into agricultural city-states, we had a radically new mode of production. Intensive agriculture replaced horticulture as the main way of producing food and fiber. That happened on Earth for a number of complex historical and cultural reasons, but wherever the economy was based on agricultural production that could produce surpluses, we got a certain kind of division of labor. Whether we look at ancient Egypt, the cultures of the Tigris and Euphrates, India, or Central America, we find kingship that is considered divinely instituted, a priest class that generally supports the kingly lineages and has a near monopoly on literacy, a warrior class, a merchant-artisan class, and a peasant class, which includes the majority of the people.

If you've looked at this discussion critically, at least two questions may have come to mind. Why do we not speak of the religion and power domains as "mirroring" each other? Or, for that matter, the communal and economic domains? And, if tribal culture was organized mainly by kinship relationships like those of the Hopi clans, why don't we speak of power relationships as being centered in the communal domain—in the clans?

Since this book is not aimed at specialists, I'll avoid some of the thornier aspects of these questions—which require a fairly extensive consideration of cultural types, variations in modes of production, and cultural interactions, mostly through the institutionalization of war. In simplest terms, the domains of the expression axis and of the ordering axis are not mirroring each other because in most real cultures they contend with each other—like the opposing poles of a bar magnet. They need not in principle, but they normally do. If cultural synergy is high, that is, if the culture allows people to comprehend and follow effective core-need strategies, the poles of the expression and ordering axes are balanced, so to speak. Because of the psychosocial exclusion principle, the strong tendency for cultures to endorse relational- or objective-mode knowing, but not both, that sort of balance is rare. I am inclined to think it is sometimes much better in simple relational cultures, however.

As a historical fact, in most societies evolved in complexity beyond the band or tribal level, religion and the temporal power hierarchy have contended with each other, and communal and economic needs have been antagonistic. They have struggled with each other, so to speak, for the energy of ordering or of expression. Of course, power hierarchies remain entangled with their legitimation by religion—even in modern, secular societies. Listen to a little bit of political rhetoric if you don't believe that. But, in fact, when the balance of relational and objective knowing fails, as it has in all modern societies, the relational and objective domains are in continuous, antagonistic interaction—a dialectic. The same is true for the communal and economic domains. Economy overwhelms community. Both ordering and expressive energy are nearly monopolized on the objective-mode side of the Brenden Matrix. The struggle in England between the power of the Roman Church and the temporal power of the monarchy was resolved by subjugating the power of the church to the temporal power. After Henry VIII, there was still a legitimation of monarchy by the new Church of England, but the monarchy could keep the power of religion in check.

What has happened historically because of that psychosocial exclusion principle we've talked about so often has been a shift toward the dominance of objective-mode social worlds. Western culture is objective-mode culture. In our modern social worlds, the energy in the expressive and the ordering dimensions of our lives has become seriously unbalanced to the right, toward the objective, toward rationality and planning and away from intuition and feeling. Thus, the ordering of social roles in terms of power relationships dominates almost every aspect of our lives. And the structure of these relationships, whether we speak of social classes or even of gender-role inequities, has mirrored the mode of production. Power in a modern, corporate society is about who has access to the resources of production, profits, and credit. Social-class inequities resonate mainly to that differential access. If you are familiar with the insights of Marx's thought, you are seeing similar understandings, although out of a different frame of reference.

In America, the domain of family and community and of institutionalized religion are drained of much of their energy. They are relational institutions in societies dominated by the objective mode of knowing. They still tend to mirror each other, especially if one takes particular ethnic or regional areas into consideration. For Italian Americans, for example, the church is still, to some extent, a legitimator of norms and values in the family. But institutionalized religion is a relatively weak force in modern societies, and nuclear families are fragments of communities. Through most of human history, the marital dyad was imbedded in extended clan relationships, in a band or village where personal relationships were the fabric of daily life. The isolated nuclear family is mainly a product of Western individualism and the industrial mode of production. Factory owners don't want to deal with children, much less uncles, aunts, and grandmothers; they want a mobile, expendable pool of workers devoted to the company, not to their family or clan or tribe.

As to the second question (since we certainly see power struggles in families), why weren't tribal clans the centers of power? Well, in fact they were, in a way, but that power was enabling or consensual, not based so much on who could tell whom what to do. The Hopi way in such things is summed up, even today, in the phrase, "cooperation without submission." Historically, however, there was still a need for a power structure not necessarily connected to kinship. That appeared in ceremonial societies in Hopi culture or among affiliations of elders or chiefs from different lineages (or even different tribes), as among the Plains Indians during their wars with the whites in the nineteenth century.

But there is another subtlety here, and it is critical to what this chapter is for. Any social institution will tend very strongly to develop social roles that echo the fourfold structure of our core needs. In fact, the fourfold structuring of human consciousness lends a property called self-recursiveness to matrix sets at every level of human activity. From married couples to institutions to whole societies, the fourfold structuring appears and reappears.

FIGURE 3: FOUR TYPES OF SOCIAL ROLES REFLECTING
THE CORE NEEDS

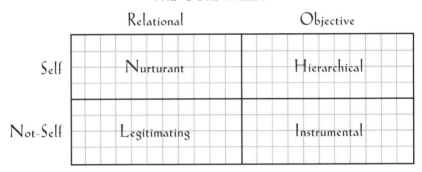

There are hierarchical or power roles, nurturant roles, instrumental roles, and legitimating roles in any institution. In fact, these four roles tend to get played by somebody wherever human groups form.

In the medieval church, for example, the nurturant (feeling) role was played mostly by the parish priest—although he was a "father" and not a "mother" because Western culture is suffused with recessive patriarchal "cultigens." Theological sages like Augustine or Nicholas of Cusa—often living in monasteries—played the (intuitive-insightful) legitimating roles. In the political hierarchy of the medieval church, bishops, archbishops, cardinals, and the pope represented the hierarchy of power roles—a fact reflected by the power of the bishop on a chessboard. Finally, the instrumental-economic and housekeeping roles were often institutionalized under a church sexton, who sometimes worked closely with a church architect in the case of parishes or districts that had cathedrals. That was because cathedrals took generations to build. Sextons were assisted by the paid or voluntary labor of artisans, laity, or overworked deacons. In a modern church the sexton is the equivalent of a janitor, reminding us that instrumental roles, the business of fixing meals, scrubbing pots, and keeping the fire going are often pushed to the bottom of social-status hierarchies. One may reasonably wonder at the justice of this practice.

In an idealized notion of the modern family, fast taking on all the reality of a Disney fantasy, women dominate the expression axis, with the burden of nurturance and instrumental labor falling to them, while husbands dominate the ordering axis, both as the "head of the house" and the legitimator of family norms and values.

In the Roman Republic, where we get a lot of our "cultural DNA" for the "father knows best" ideal in modern culture, the *pater familias* was not only legal head of the house, but was also the head priest of the family hearth deities, the *lares* and *penates*.

Of course, in modern societies, where all goods and services are valued as commodities under the spell of money, women increasingly must work outside the home. This shift in the mode of production has had the effect of shattering the already unstable ideal of nuclear families and is pure hell on children.

OF MASKS AND FACES

Understanding how the four types of roles can be managed in your personal struggle toward self-knowing is intimately related to understanding how we can overcome our personal ego strategies. The four roles can be played out of ego or out of self-awareness. Nurturant roles can either sustain people and give vital energy to human life or be perverted by the common and destructive business of making guilty. There are Jewish mothers in all cultures; some of them are men who aren't even Jewish. Hierarchical roles can order for the common good, allowing us to pursue collective goals, or attempt to monopolize the life energy of others through fear and intimidation. Instrumental roles can be symbiotic, in harmony with the life energy of other species and of the Earth system, or destructive and exploitative. Legitimating roles may empower or they may project blame, guilt, and fear.

The four general types of social roles are related to ego strategies because we are sociable creatures. Our "life movies" roll along in the give and take of social interaction, even when that interaction is contaminated by nonproductive internal dialogues between "takes." And the need strategies we use depend on the social role we are playing as well as on the focus of our personal consciousness.

There is no such thing as personal salvation; we save each other. Your journey to the self—or mine—does not take place on an island somewhere, but in the office and in the mall, in the bedroom and in commuter traffic. We all have to learn the relational arts "on the job," together. It was Sartre who said that "hell is other people." So is heaven.

But for the rest of this chapter, let's take a quick tour of hell. That is, let's look at how the function paths work in the ego.

How Function Paths Work in the Ego: An Introduction to Scarcity Egonomics

Ego action is inversion of self-action. When we act out of the ego we are trying to get what we want through attack and defense based in insecurity—which is experienced as fear even when we do not give it that name. The human experience of fear, of isolation, of alienation, is assured in any social world where the natural self is attacked by guilt strategies (which will be explained shortly) and where methods of cosmic grounding (organized religion, for example) are weakly integrated into actual personal experience and the need for cosmic grounding is not understood.

In your life and mine, all of this horribleness begins with a process called primary socialization. That elemental cosmic disaster takes place, usually, before we are six, mostly before we are four. During this induction into our local consensus trance, we learn our basic strategies for dealing with insecurity. That is, we form an ego.

The insecurity comes initially from finding the self caught in a body in time. According to esoteric knowledge, your higher self, your soul, has selected the "Earth experience." But if we are to credit such sources, discovering we are caught in a tiny locality in space time is still a huge shock.

If our social worlds had high synergy, if the core needs were well understood and the modes of knowing held in a balance, socialization would not be what it is in Western culture. But that is not the way it is.

In unbalanced consensus realities, the ego forms around guilt, which is an attack on the self, and shame, which is feeling bad because we learn to believe we deserve these self-attacks. Guilt and shame are misplaced life energy. The basic pattern works like this: As tiny children we are physically vulnerable and dependent on the goodwill of our caregivers. To get our diapers changed, get fed, cuddled, sung to, and played with, we typically learn to read the body language, tone of voice, and—certainly by age four—the meanings of spoken language around us. We develop a world image by the interaction in our consciousness of four meaning categories. That world image is mainly organized around language. All language acts to limit and condition our perception. It teaches us to see the world at second hand by agreeing that what we can name exists and what we cannot name probably does not exist, save "in our imaginations." The world image can be expressed as a matrix set that contains:

An affective or emotional body.	A cognitive map spun of words and symbols.
A valuative map of what's "good" or "bad."	A conditioned sensory guide to pleasure/pain.

In the sensory realm we learn that there are some things around us that give pleasure and others that give pain. The cat's fur is nice, Dad's beard stubble hurts, the sunlight feels good, having wet hair feels yucky.

In the realm of thinking, we begin to form a reality map or cognitive map as we learn language. At first, anyway, the meanings of the words we learn are associated directly to what things are for. (We associate an object form with a function.) Food is for eating, beds for sleeping, butterflies for chasing. We also learn which things are "me" and which are "not-me." My nose is "me"; the doorknob isn't. Later we learn about abstraction and general concepts like momentum and the square root of four, but the form-to-function association comes first and it lingers. The first thing a student will ask about a quadratic equation—if his or her natural child has not been totally overwhelmed—is "What do you do with it?"

In the affective or feeling domain of our consciousness, we become aware of our world as having to do either with fear or with love. Perhaps we start out by taking unconditional love for granted, but unless our caregivers are remarkable indeed, the lapses in that first assumption become associated with insecurity and fear. For many of us there are lots of lapses. You may recall that Plato's *Republic* was to shelter and nurture children, away from the full shock of the rough-and-tumble of society, for a number of years. Your parents and mine had to take care of us in the midst of their own battles for self-worth, making a living, and getting the love *they* needed.

In the valuative domain, we learn the difference between feeling guilty and feeling good about ourselves. Just how that happens will be explained shortly.

On the expression axis of our core needs, fear gets linked to pain and love gets linked to pleasure. On the ordering axis, "me" actions and "not-me" actions, real or imagined, get linked to "good" or "bad." That is, our actions in the world—or the actions of others, or even of nature—are either legitimated or repudiated as "good" or "bad." Along the way, it should be noted by anyone who has raised a child, we quickly learn to project "me" actions as "good" and blame "not-me" actions for our grievous errors. You can see how these connections look in Figure 4.

FIGURE 4: EXPRESSION AND ORDERING PATHS
IN PRIMARY SOCIALIZATION

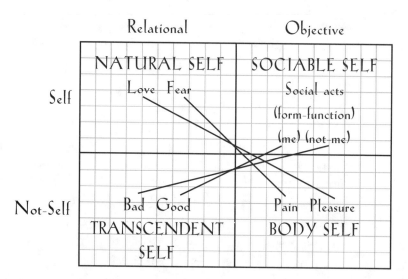

The associations we see in Figure 4 are how our function paths (the primary links between psychic functions and core needs discussed at the beginning of this chapter) look as the ego is forming. The mirror paths are also operating, of course, although I've left connecting lines out to reduce clutter. On the relational side, the mirror path links our sense of what is "good" to our sense of love, while what we think of as "bad" tends to reflect fear.

On the objective side of the matrix, there is a general tendency for pleasure or pain to be associated with the purposes or functions of things. At the same time, pain tends to become a "not-me" association and pleasure a "me" association. We like to "own" our pleasures and dissociate from what hurts.

So far, so good. The problem, the ego, starts with the fact that what we do is always in a social context, in a social world with rules we have to learn to get our needs met. If the rules are conflicted, as they are in Western social worlds, we share a problem. The shadow (where we hide the "naughty" parts of our natural self), the mask (which we hold up to others to give them a good impression), the body image (the idea we form about how our body looks to others), and the superego (where we store guilt) take their form in us as we interact with others.

Here's an example of the basic way blessed things get contaminated, how the self learns to believe it is an ego. I see a cookie on a plate and experience desire. The expression axis is doing its thing. Life energy flows from our desire nature to our actions. In the individual psyche, all action starts on the axis of sensation and feeling. We try to avoid pain and get pleasure. Freud was right about that, up to a point. Our actions or expressions in the world are also about extending love (life energy) and expecting to receive it.

Since I've had a cookie before and already associate cookies with pleasure, I take a cookie from the plate—an action coordinated out of my cognitive map of what's in the world and what cookies are for. The cookie tastes good. Pleasure. Yep, that's a cookie. (Reinforcement happens. The behaviorist models have part of the picture, too.) But pleasure, remember, is linked to our need for love. In fact, the connection of eating and nurturance is well known—even when the connection is symbolic, as in the Eucharistic feast on the body and blood of Christ.

Now. Let's say Mom yells at us halfway through the cookie. The pleasure-love path is aborted. If you think of that path as having a certain energy, remembering that energy simply gets transformed, not done away with, where does the energy go? To the budding superego. The superego is our guilt-storage bin. The "bad" action of eating the forbidden cookie is now "stored" as an association between the action thwarted and the deflected energy— now experienced as guilt. From then on, forbidden-cookie eating is associated with stored guilt on the developing ego's ordering axis. Of course, where "aborted" life energy gets stored, in fact, is mysterious. It is not in a little box. My guess is that deflected energy is partly carried in conflicted neurophysiological imprinting—in our brain and body-chemistry patterns—and in the energy body that organizes the physical body, particularly in the aspect of that entity called the "emotional body."

In any case, how does "good" energy become "bad"? By having a "bad" definition applied to it. The desire energy remains the same. That's why guilt may actually seem to enhance pleasure and why it breaks away from the ordering axis like a stored electrical charge from a capacitor, one way or another, like it or not. Freud observed this phenomenon as the inevitable return of repressed psychic material. Here we will simply call it "compensation." Stored energy gets expressed, sooner or later, somehow or other. In fact, just about all our core-need strategies when expressed through the ego are strained through guilt resistors. Just about everything we do is about trying to "deserve love."

Can the aborted definition get redefined, releasing that energy? Sure. It is possible to eat cookies or even have sex without guilt. Generally, however, as with forbidden masturbation, we keep seeking the pleasure because it's stronger than the guilt. We don't necessarily get rid of the guilt, but we do learn to confuse the guilt with pleasure. Hence, "guilty pleasures," such as naughty (guilt-associated) sexual fantasies.

In any case, if we really could consciously redefine guilt-associated desires, if we had the awareness to see the core need behind them, this chapter would end here. It doesn't.

CONTROL DRAMAS

Let's get down to the problem of control dramas made famous lately in a best-seller called *The Celestine Prophecy*. A control drama, as author James Redfield explains it, is our customary way of getting the life energy we need by stealing it from others. According to his interview with Michael Toms on a recent "New Dimensions" radio broadcast, he got this idea initially from existential psychologist Ronald Laing.[1] In his model we may play *poor me* (which is making guilty), become an *interrogator* (which is a strategy for finding fault in another in order to project blame), an *intimidator* (who steals energy directly by making another fearful) or, simply, *remain aloof* (which is actually trying to make others guilty for not paying attention to us).

We steal energy from others through power games because we don't think we can get it directly, through a higher awareness or consciousness state. Redfield proposes that we can "clear" our control dramas by becoming aware of how our parents, for example, stole energy from us. If your dad was an "interrogator," for example, you might adopt an "aloofness" strategy—part withdrawal, part see-how-detached-and-in-need-of-nurturance-I-am. By becoming aware that your drama is a response to a complementary one, you can drop your aloofness strategy.

Now, Redfield's and Laing's notion here is important. We do, indeed, try to get the life energy we need from each other. Many of us certainly experience ourselves as hurting and empty and ready to drain anyone we can of all the real or imagined unconditional love we can get from them. And (as long as we identify with our ego) we use a variety of ego strategies to do that. And, yes—as Redfield has it in one of his nine insights—we can learn

to draw love-life-energy "direct." That's what the process of individuation and the journey to the self are all about. But matrix
theory suggests a different model of how all of this happens and
what to do about ego strategies of all sorts.

First of all, the scarring in us pretty much always starts with
stored guilt. We learn to see ourselves as unworthy of love and
spend an enormous amount of time and energy trying to feel
worthy of love from then on.

We don't get the life energy we need because we don't think
we deserve it. In Pogo Possum's immortal words, "We has met
the enemy and they is us."

So that's the key. The trick is to get free enough of ego consciousness so that we can re-discover our innocence, our worthiness
to give and receive love—which is how we get energy directly.
That's what self-honesty and paying attention are for. But can we
do that simply by discovering our control dramas? Will that allow
us to become aware of our actual core needs and evade the business
of the ego—which is compensating for stored guilt energy?

Not entirely. Here's why. It is not simply a particular control
drama that resonates to guilt, it is the entire ordering axis. That
means the ego ideal (our imagined ideal self) is energized *in total*
from the aborted, stored energy of the superego. The ego ideal is
the compensating mechanism of the superego, of our stored
guilt. Life energy continues to flow along the ego's expression
axis, from the shadow to the body image and back again, but it
becomes a weak signal, full of static. (Which is why we so often
feel deprived when we're in ordinary ego-level consciousness.)

How we present ourselves to others is a sort of endless apology,
even if we don't have Jewish mothers. That's one of the first things
radical self-honesty begins to discover. Of course, sometimes, in a
process called ego inflation, our endless apology becomes a great
huffing and puffing. Ego strutting. These peacock antics would be
ridiculous, comical, if they were not often taken so seriously. But
compensation by apology sometimes gets a temporary boost from
someone who compensates by ego inflation, especially if the

inflated one can seem to help off-load some guilt and hatred toward any target prejudice and bigotry may supply.

Also, our efforts to get the life energy we need are slippery. The "control drama" we use is a function of the social role we are playing and actually can draw on the full range of defenses—denial, rationalization, projection, repression, and so on. Maybe I should repeat that.

The ego strategy we use to get the life energy we need depends on the type of social role we are playing.

Therefore, while we may favor one sort of ego strategy over another, we probably use all of them. While we play a nurturant role under the influence of the shadow, we play make-guilty. Holding up our social mask, compensating for guilt, we mainly off-load blame through projection, faultfinding, or other sorts of implicit or explicit power games. We may consciously or unconsciously employ instrumental roles to carry out destructive agendas for a number of odd reasons. Rebelling against the feeling that we are "being used," we "accidentally" burn the roast when the boss comes to dinner. (Destructive action may be intentional without being conscious.) Or, to get even with an abusive foreman, we "pretend to work" on the assembly line. To make ourselves hard and impervious to pain, we may even become efficient killers for the Foreign Legion.

Finally, we may use our legitimating roles to make lots of people insecure and fearful—which is the sinister side of "experts" in every field. Our entire conventional medical system resonates to this sort of strategy, even if the individual players are idealistic and well intentioned.

Also, even though Redfield's suggestion that we find the "silver lining" in the damage done to us by our parents isn't trivial—we can gradually become aware of what life challenges we have selected in concert with other souls—it is simply not practical to do that by remembering our parents' control dramas.

You can figure out your parents' control dramas. You'll probably find that they are still playing them and they still hurt. But you cannot undo your parents' behavior; that is not your responsibility. Even if you could, that in itself would not undo your scarring. An awful lot of the deflected guilt energy in us gets "down-loaded" from aborted pleasure-love paths while we are very small. You may think about how your mother treated you, but you are not likely ever to learn much about the role of the day-care worker who nurtured you (or didn't) when you were three.

Our neurophysiology—the configuration of musculature, metabolism, conditioned response patterns—is probably imprinted with some of our early "guilt work." And some of that damage may be accessible to skillful body work, to touch therapies. But our ego foundation gets laid before we can think about it with words. The power your parents—or others—had to make you feel unworthy of love and, therefore, powerless to give it, is built into your ego. Your parents deserve no judgment for this. Their faulty core-need strategies came from the scarring they got from their parents and so on and on.

So. What then can we do about our feelings of unworthiness, stored guilt, and the resulting craziness of the ego?

Nothing.

That is, nothing when we are in ego consciousness. We never solve a problem out of the consciousness in which it is produced. The way out of scarcity egonomics is the rediscovery of abundance beyond reckoning. And that only takes place by tuning our awareness to a different frequency, to a different "consciousness frequency." The sense of isolation, insecurity, and our perpetual need to guard, defend, and attack is inherent in what the ego is for. The ego cannot be revised, edited, or abridged in any ultimately useful way while we are operating out of its assumptions.

Those assumptions will be considered in the next chapter. They have this in common: they are all lies.

The ego's triad is:

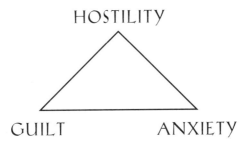

These correspond to our perceptions of past, present, and future. But, in the dynamics of the ego, we are never in the present. It cannot exist.

The triad of the self is:

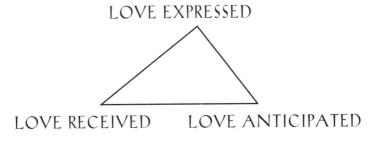

In the holy trinity of the self there are no dimensions of time. In the awareness of the self, we do not dwell in time, but in three moments ever present.

7

Of Masks and Faces: Life in the Consensus Trance

When people lost sight of the way to live,
Came codes of love and honesty,
Learning came, charity came,
Hypocrisy took charge,
When differences weakened family ties
Came benevolent fathers and dutiful sons,
And when lands were disrupted and misgoverned
Came ministers commended as loyal.

Lao Tzu, the eighteenth saying of the *Tao Te Ching*

Like T. S. Eliot's hollow men, heads stuffed with straw, we wander through our days, entranced by a story we tell ourselves. The story is not even a lie, it is simply a dream. To make the dream seem true, we share it. But our sharing is a whispering among shadows, an emptiness agreed on. The world we have made for our dreaming is dim-witted and cruel, for we have heaped scorn and spite on the knowing that comes without words, or before them—the knowing of the heart, of insight. We honor objective knowing, which is about things set apart, and forget the language of things connected. We have learned to live all alone in our heads, forgetting the dance of hearts joined.

THE CONSENSUS TRANCE

The dream we share, the dream that makes up any social word, is spun of ghostly fibers in this way. We are born into vulnerable bodies and delivered into the river of time. That trauma is accommodated in us by developing a defensive structure we call the ego. But the ego is a contingent thing, dependent on a sharing of assumptions, the assumptions of our local consensus reality. Like the rest of a social world, the ego is a negotiated settlement. We make a bargain. Out of the apparently fatally compromised power of the natural self, we bargain away our authenticity, the power of our natural self, in exchange for survival. We agree to surrender direct knowing for partial, sec- ondhand knowing, which is given its form, for the most part, by language and symbol.

Learning the language of our local culture is the equivalent of ingesting a provincial word map that tells us what is real and what is not. This map, the heart of our world image, teaches us what is "thinkable" and what is "unthinkable." Since language is the medium of the thinking function in us and often a stranger in the relational domains of the self, we are often taught that questions "unthinkable" are the dominion of poets, sages, prophets, and mystics—none of whom are practical enough to have "common sense." Since all of these social types must cope with the consensus trance, that may be true. Poets and mystics may well be maladapted to the local social world.

The process of being inducted into a consensus reality proceeds as the learning of language teaches us to name some things but not others. Things not named tend not even to be noticed. When things without names are forced into our awareness, we may think ourselves deluded. If we report these experiences, our fellows may assure us that we are deluded and, possibly, offer to burn us at the stake for the good of our "immortal souls," or attempt to "cure" us with some other punishment, such as those offered in psychiatric wards. In any case, the language we learn inevitably conditions our neurophysiology along with the musculature and characteristic postures of the body. Depending on how they are enculturated, people respond differently to natural circadian rhythms, to temperature differences, and even to colors. They walk differently, smile at slightly different cues, laugh and cry for different reasons. And there, of course, is the apparently irreconcilable paradox of the human condition, the tragedy of culture. Enculturation incarcerates us. Thereafter, we know the language of fellow inmates, but not the languages of our common, inherent power, or of our natural, shared human freedom.

In terms of function paths, here is how this happens. First, as we are socialized, our body state, our neurological functioning, mirrors the conditioning of perception by language. We learn to "see" certain colors and shapes more readily than others, for example. We learn that it is more comfortable to sit in a chair or to hunker on our heels. As this happens, the expression axis (the link between our feeling and sensation functions) becomes established because any perception (in fact, any body state) has an affective component. We feel something, however subtle, about walking, sitting, folding our arms, about the words for "mother," "butterfly," "peanut butter," or even the color "red." Figure 1 recalls how the expression axis is represented in the Brenden Matrix.

FIGURE 1: THE EXPRESSION AXIS REPRESENTED IN THE BRENDEN MATRIX

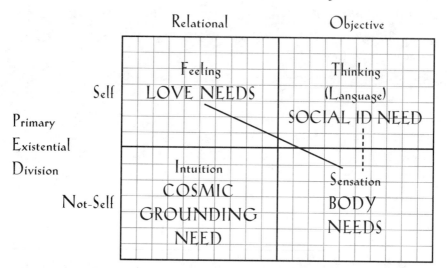

Mode of Knowing

In Figure 1, the diagonal line represents the function path that links our feeling and sensation functions as well as our needs for giving and receiving love and our need for body nurturance. The dotted line represents the mirror path that links conditioned (language-coded) perception to our body's neurophysiology. In effect (starting with the dotted line), conditioned perception, mainly through language (which tells us what is "thinkable" and what is "unthinkable"), conditions how we see, hear, smell, taste, feel, and interpret the world around us. Because this happens, the expression axis is made less "open." We get used to certain "familiar" body states associated with "proper" thought categories, and, therefore, to certain feeling states. This is inevitable since body states correlate to feeling states. Every emotion we have (at least while we are in-physical) corresponds to billions of biochemical reactions amid the billions of cells swarming in the organizing energy field we call our body. Conditioned perception, because it limits our body as an information-receiving-and-expression vehicle, has the effect of constraining our feeling nature, restricting our "affective repertoire." In short, in the link between our need for giving and receiving love and our need to tend to our body, some neurophysiological responses are encouraged by cultural norms; some are not. Therefore, we are open to certain kinds of feelings and not to others.

Cultural repression of our potential for feeling and for using our bodies as vehicles of expression may have relatively simple effects, like forbidding us to hug a friend of the same sex. But the limitations may be far more profound. We may teach ourselves to be afraid of the feelings associated with a light trance state or even quiet meditation, since these states are not "familiar." In this way, we cut off an avenue away from the ego into the self. We may learn to mistrust or ignore what may be learned from whole domains of consciousness, like our dream states. For example, among the Senoi of Malaysia, children are taught not only how to be aware of their dreams, but how to enter into them and learn lessons about reality through a process called lucid dreaming (in which you are conscious of being in a dream state and able to manipulate it). In our culture, some people have lucid dreams spontaneously, but they are probably less frequent (or less frequently remembered) than among the Senoi. More to the point, when you have a lucid dream, you are less likely to know "how to think" about it, *and* it may make you feel "creepy" or uncomfortable. It doesn't "fit" in your social world. Therefore, you will be far less likely to receive the gifts of dreaming.

Constraints on our capacity to see and to feel the world around us have a lot to do with our unhappiness. With little understanding of the power of the natural self, for example, we teach our children to stop playing and assume the postures and attitudes of grief when attending a funeral. In all kinds of social situations, in fact, children are taught when to laugh, when not to laugh, and often directed in the same moment that neither is appropriate. Soon they learn that the passive frown is a sign of thoughtfulness. Such a facial expression becomes "comfortable" as deep sadness begins to shadow the remorseless business of doing what is expected.

Meanwhile, the ordering axis that links our thinking and intuition functions—our need for social identity and for cosmic grounding—generally begins to accommodate chronic imbalance. (Take a look at Figure 1 and imagine a diagonal path between the upper right and lower left quadrants. This is what we call the ordering axis.) Since the only world we are permitted or expected to believe in is the consensus reality, and especially in Western culture, as we learn to mistrust feeling and intuition, we learn to feel that social acceptability *is* cosmic grounding. We may come to believe that the right job, the proper income, and the right car are as much grounding in the universe as anyone can expect.

At that point, the psychosocial exclusion principle has done its wicked work. We are entranced by our culture's insistence on emphasizing the objective mode of knowing and devaluing the relational. As the ego takes its form in us under these conditions, the energy of our desire nature is "downloaded" as guilt to shroud the transcendent face of the self, to replace our actual cosmic grounding with the leering condemnation of the superego. We learn to walk in numbing cadences to the metronome of local time. We become strangers in a strange land who have lost our passports to the timelessness at the foundation of the self. We learn to live with the more or less permanent exhaustion of "self-lag."

HELL'S LABYRINTH

So we see that the awkward minuet of egos, yours and mine, is inseparable from the nature of the social world that is the master of the somber dance. A mother scolding a child in a shopping mall is about the frustration of a mother, the fury of a child thwarted, and about the meaning of shopping malls. The jaded indifference of a Chicano teenager in the back of an algebra class is about anger, denial, projection, social-class inequities, survival of the fittest, racism, denial of death, underpaid teachers, corrupted school boards, sham and pretense, normative lying, the fading dreams of the American middle class, and multinational corporations exporting labor-intensive manufacturing jobs to cut costs and increase profits.

We may not believe this, of course. We may not believe that our personal problems and failings are intertwined with the nature of our shared social worlds, that a failed love affair is connected to social patterns as well as to ego games. That is partly because of the ego assumptions we mentioned in the preceding chapter.

The tacit, mainly unconscious, assumptions on which our ego consciousness is founded are not solely personal, although we may entertain them in distinctive ways. In fact, they are shared to an astonishing degree by nearly everyone in our social world. A consensus trance, by definition, is a shared trance.

NEWTON'S TRIANGLE

Here are the typical assumptions underlying and built into ego-level consciousness for most people socialized into Western culture.

1. Materialism. Everything that's really real is matter. It is detectable by the senses and measurable on a scale. What is not measurable by the senses is not real, or has only secondary reality and is dependent on matter. The mind is thought to be "in" the brain, for example.

2. Objectivism. All the world is divided into separate parts. I am in my body; you are in yours. The world is made out of moving parts—atoms, molecules, Hondas. The part you are responsible for—your body—has no necessary connection to anyone or anything else. Objectivism in America is strongly associated with two social myths that are part of the collective ego: survival of the fittest in a war of all against all, and competitive, radical individualism.

3. Determinism. All real events are material (measurable matter-energy) events that have material causes. Nothing that is not measurable as some expression of matter-energy (like your experience of existing) has any actual existence. In this classical scientific model, all these matter-energy events, like reactions between molecules of water vapor or between neurotransmitters in your brain, are linked in an inevitable chain of cause and effect, beginning with some mysterious uncaused cause. In such a world view, your every action is predetermined by an inevitable chain of prior material causes. Your sexuality, your feelings about your mother, your belief in an afterlife are all mere effects of atoms and molecules interacting with each other. Out of such a model of reality, of course, free will is an illusion and the contents of your mind only an effect of the molecules in your brain. What you think, feel, and experience in this classical view are merely subjective and, finally, more or less irrelevant.

A corollary of determinism is reductionism. If we break something into its parts, we will understand what it is. Try breaking up your desire nature into parts and you get the approach to human nature known as molecular biology. (That's the discipline that tries to discover how serotonin, norepinephrine, and other complex organic molecules, called neurotransmitters, are related to feelings and cognitions.) The findings of molecular biologists don't necessarily have to be used out of deterministic assumptions. Feelings, including intent or will, can be thought of as correlated and complementary to body states, for example. Mostly, though, molecular biology is reductionistic and materialistic.[1]

None of the three underlying assumptions making up Newton's triangle tend to be conscious; they are primarily unconscious; they are built into our cognitive map of the world image when we are very young. David Bohm called such ideas the "thoughts with which we think."[2]

Newton's Triangle arose with Western rationalism and science. And here is its built-in paradox: all of its assumptions have been essentially demolished by science. For sociological (not scientific) reasons, some scientists haven't gotten the word yet. Traditional scientific thinking clings to the old assumptions. The implications of research into the indeterminism inherent in complex systems; the nature of relativistic fields as a continuum of probabilities (not "hard facts"); nonlocal connection in quantum physics; and "nonmaterial" causes of "material effects"—as in prayer effects on healing—have not soaked in yet (see Chapter 10 for an example of such a study). The assumptions of Newton's Triangle are not about what is real and true. They are, ultimately, useful (but limited) frames of reference peculiar to that historical creature we call Western culture.

Meanwhile, what we need to understand here is that Newton's triangle is a form that conditions our perception and the nature of social worlds to an amazing degree.

Out of the swamp of these mostly hidden assumptions come the nightmare creatures of our daily lives, the toxic revengers. If we are not quite sure how to name them, we know them by their ghoulish forms, their mannequin smiles, their stench. We tell each other stories about them. Ego lore.

THE PRINCIPLES OF SCARCITY EGONOMICS

DEATH IS THE END OF EVERYTHING

Although the main way we deal with death out of ego-level consciousness is by denial, even while we are forced to deal with it from time to time, the fear of death remains as a sort of opaque, light-absorbing backdrop to our lives. Every happy scene is tinged with a certain poignancy, a hint of sadness. The young lovers will grow old or fall out of love. For every wedding, there is a funeral, for every birth, a death certificate. Illness, losing a job, getting divorced, are little deaths that sound a faint, haunting tocsin reminding us of the final death. The graveyard and the clock are the somber sentinels of our fleeting days.

So profound is the power of death in Western culture that beliefs about transcendence, survival, reincarnation, and resurrection are hedged about with incredulity and doubt. Sigmund Freud, sounding a dismal chord that echoes yet through the corridors of our hurried passing, assured us that religion was an infantile projection, and rumors of angels but empty tales for frightened children. Citing the poet Heine, he bid us leave heaven "to the angels and the sparrows," and charged us with the grave responsibility of tending to rational matters and accepting our mortality.[3] Only science, Newtonian science, could offer any hope.

Freud's world image resonates to Newton's triangle, but he is no anomaly. From Jean Paul Sartre to Woody Allen, the dismal certainty that our lives flow away from us on a river of time remains a fundamental assumption. For many thoughtful people it seems the only reasonable assumption.

Where the power of death is denied, from pulpits, from theological tracts, the messages often have a hollow, uncertain timbre. Our public denials of death are ringed about with leering doubt. When, in my youthful idealism, I explored the possibility of attending a famous theological seminary, thinking I might find some threshold there in my quest for meaning, I found that most of the seminarians had no vital, experientially grounded faith in personal survival.

On the other hand, fundamentalist credos about the mystery behind the crypt seem fearful, defensive, and too often linked to precarious bands of the elect—barely distinguishable in their consciousness or their behavior from the hordes of the damned. Religion wrapped in odd, secondhand tales of a patriarchal God, inscrutable, cruel judgment, lakes of fire, rapture, and resurrected corpses is a pretty thin spiritual gruel. Even for those who are ready to surrender their minds to the appeal of being acceptable to a band of believers, it is a shoddy substitute for cosmic grounding.

Our core need for knowing we are at home and safe in the cosmos can only be informed by relational knowing, by feeling and, especially, by intuition. Death's meaning for us cannot unfold from mere thinking, from words, intellectual formulations, or beliefs of any kind. We can only know what we know. What we do not know by direct encounter that illuminates the heart of our questioning is not an answer, it is simply an empty surmise. Recall that if there is a question that sums up our cosmic grounding concern, it might be "Is the universe friendly?" A universe that does not answer is not friendly.

Newton's triangle assures us that we are only bodies adrift in the random vagaries of things that just happen in space and time. Orgasms happen, shit happens, death happens. Materialism, objectivism, and determinism assure our faith in death and deny the mystery of life. Death is the ultimate prosecutor of our search for fulfillment, meaning, and joy. We cannot stand up to its cross-examinations in the court of the ego. Which, of course, is a final, critical commentary on ego-think, for undoing an inappropriate fear of death is central to self-awareness. It is so critical that it will concern us in some detail in Chapter 10.

Our faith in death is the ultimate power of the superego's pale shroud over the transcendent face of the self. For, if we are honest in our inner search, eventually we encounter the deep suspicion that we die because we deserve to die. Death is the sanctum sanctorum with no mystery inside save the void, the darkness that has no form, the emptiness that has no beginning and no end. It is also, it seems, our inevitable destiny.

To the extent that we honor a faith in death, we are asleep to the power of life, which is the only power we have. Fortunately, it seems, that power is more than sufficient. But until the awesome dawn of that understanding begins to break across the horizon of our knowing, the flow of love through our lives remains a weak trickle over the seemingly implacable dam of insecurity and fear, the obstruction of guilt and self-condemnation we here call the superego.

The corollaries of faith in death drift like the debris of a wrecked ship into all of the other aspects of the ego. We loathe aging and worship youth, wreaking havoc with our body image. Isolated in our little cage of time, we learn to fight viciously for whatever power we can wrest from others, staving off the inevitable catastrophe of self-annihilation as long as possible. Compensation-for-guilt, the blueprint for our ego ideal, resonates to the fear of death. Worst of all, in my view, we learn to fear intimacy, to doubt our natural drive to love and to be loved. Which brings us to the next principle of scarcity egonomics.

INNOCENCE IS WEAKNESS

Every social world has ways and means of keeping the natural self in check, although most relational cultures are not so repressive as ours. In Western culture, we mainly hobble the natural self by casting doubt and loathing on Eros and its attendants. And, of course, we do that by making guilty. We end up with a powerfully conflicted inner directive that is also a basic principle of scarcity egonomics. The principle has two conflicted parts:

1. Happiness is pleasure and the avoidance of pain.

2. It is well and proper to doubt the virtue of our pleasures and to feel we deserve the pain. The only way out of this prime misdirective is the re-visioning of our innocence.

Actually, the deepest longing in us is for joy, of which our fleeting pleasures are but echoes. Joy is not contingent; it has no necessary relationship whatever to the objective conditions of our lives at any moment. Joy and peace are aspects of our ground state. On the other hand, while we live in bodies and watch clocks, the quest for pleasure, generally centering on the body's comfort, is understandable. We are on Earth to experience being in a body in time and to share earthy things. Because the natural self is sensual, denying ourselves rest and other bodily pleasures both attacks the self and reduces our ability to be compassionate. Although there is value in disciplines of withdrawal from bodily comfort for a time—to discover that the body is more resilient than we imagine, to get body awareness out of the way for spiritual work—bodily asceticism as a way of living is a relational mode error, an imbalance.

Our only genuine power is in the natural self. To deny its sacred pentagram—playfulness, curiosity, sensuality, spontaneity, and sensitivity to beauty—is to disempower the self. As we begin to know what we want and, therefore, who we are, the way we experience pleasure may shift from body conditions to the joy of alignment, of allowing ourselves to be guided by our inherent desire nature. But there is no virtue in forcing the matter. Eat when you are hungry, take a nap when you are sleepy, look at clouds, dance, do inner work for the joy in it, not just as a compensation strategy.

It is through the inherent innocence of the natural self that we are channels for intimacy and for love present.

You Are All Alone

So elemental is the experience of being all alone in the brittle cage of our skulls that it is difficult for thoughtful people like us to imagine it is not, ultimately, true. We are born alone and we will die alone, goes the litany. Indeed, out of our deep entrance-ment into the materialism and objectivism of Newton's triangle, no other conclusion seems possible. Yet the quest for cosmic grounding, which is the experience of being at home and safe in the universe, is simply impossible while we hold this apparently irrefutable conviction.

You cannot discover that you are *not* alone while you are oper-ating out of the ego's assumptions. You just can't get there from here. How we can get there will concern us in Chapter 9. For now, take it as a principle of scarcity egonomics and simply recall some of its effects. If I am all alone, what I think and feel is ulti-mately meaningless. If I am all alone, what I do doesn't matter much. If I am all alone, getting pleasure from others is mainly an exercise in stroke exchange: I'll give you good feelings if you give me good feelings. But we must keep a ledger and agree on who owes whom what.

COMMODITY FETISHISM

As Wal-Mart and Kmart have become the hub of shopping malls, as the mall has replaced the town square, the things we buy sometimes seem to have become the only dependable mea-sure of who we are. We may feel we are what we believe. We cer-tainly consider our identity to be linked to the job we have. But, by and large, our consciousness of what our life is for is reflected in what we buy. People cannot often tell from looking at us that we are ardent liberals or born-again Christians. And we are not supposed to wear badges that call attention to our social status. But they can see our Mercedes.

Even when we don't sport BORN TO SHOP stickers on our rear bumpers, most of us are compulsive, addicted commodity junkies. In fact, what Marxists call "commodity fetishism" is at the very center of the scarcity egonomics of modern societies.

Since that may not be obvious, you may want to think about it a bit. Here's a way you might like to do that. While tracking your desires and paying attention to your consciousness (as we talked about in Chapter 3), think about the way your sense of freedom is linked to money. Next, think of how you feel when you think about your income's being threatened. Scared? Angry?

Probably. And with good reason.

In a money economy, dollars become like oxygen to the cells of a body. Cut down on the oxygen supply and cells start to die. In our social world, money is, literally, a matter of life and death. Social death. Physical death. Of course, commodity fetishism and the assumption that money is the ultimate standard of what is valuable are not peculiar to American society. They are complex planetary phenomena that threatens the relationship of human life to the biosphere. Looked at from an ecological-systems perspective, for example, the assumption that we can make economic hay from the remains of burned-out tropical forests is a bit like deciding we—as an integral aspect of the Earth system—can do with less and less lung tissue. (Tropical forests, of course, are Earth's year-round carbon dioxide ingesters and oxygen producers—among other vital functions.)

Closer to home, consider the astonishing insanity we discover in comparing a competitive, capitalistic economic system to any other system—like an organism (your body), an ecosystem (a marsh), or, for that matter, your personal computer. Viable systems maintain their self-organizing complexity through a balance of give and take with their environment. An organism, for example, takes in raw energy, organizes it in complex patterns of information, and then dissipates energy (waste) back into the environment. Interestingly, through billions of years of evolving progressively more complex systems, the overall Earth system has "arranged things" so that one system's waste is another system's raw material. All of this proceeds in a complex of interlocking and interacting cycles. We breathe oxygen and exhale carbon dioxide, for example. Plants breathe carbon dioxide and exude oxygen as waste. And so on. Healthy systems tend to get into balance with the systems around them.

Now, compare any healthy system with a society that has a capitalist-industrial "metabolism." This sort of social metabolism requires that commodities of all sorts, from tract houses to toothpaste, be attached to a "synthetic carrier molecule." Money. In order for the "cells" of this organiclike system (people) to get what is needed for survival and social identity—and for the over-all health of the social system—they must get into the "flow" of this "synthetic carrier molecule."

But there is a problem. The social rules of this society require the production of goods and services that can be treated as com-modities—lipstick, Chevrolets, sage medical advice, drugs, and so on and on and on. Anything that cannot be reckoned a com-modity is outside the money flow or languishing with only tiny bits of it. Children in such a system are not assets; they are expenses. And the arduous work of actually raising children seems mainly to drain away the time and energy the "social cells" need to find ways to get money.

In such a system, social status becomes associated with power prerogatives associated, in turn, with rights to commodities or to commodity tender. Money. The turn of this wicked helix directs us to sense that we are justified in estimating one person's value over another's in terms of how well they are playing the com-modity game. Assets become a measure of a person's value. Social value, and the measure of one's success in compensating for guilt, become roughly equivalent. People without assets have little or no value—except, perhaps, as ornaments or as cheap labor. We make up little tales to explain this cruelty to ourselves, to mollify our ego ideal (which is also our guilt manager). These rational-izations are often taken as a measure of how "realistic" one is.

The "just world hypothesis," brought to our attention by social psychologist Melvin J. Lerner, is characteristic of such rationalizations. It declares that in a just and orderly world, virtue is rewarded. That is, we tell ourselves, for example, that if God is good, good things should happen to good people and bad things should happen to bad people. To be sure, evidence to the contrary abounds, but rationalizations are not rational. By the law of the "just world hypothesis," people who are dying of AIDS, on welfare with no money for basic health care for their children, in prisons or mental hospitals, too young to understand the game or too old to play, are getting what they deserve. We are particularly entranced by this rationalization if we have an advantage in the social game, but not necessarily. Losers often buy the con too; they blame themselves for their "failures." Marx called this sort of rationalization, whether embraced by "winners" or "losers," "false consciousness." In fact, our little tales of inner deception are the wages of primary socialization and of embracing guilt as the energy of the ego.

Does your sensitivity rebel at this? Of course. We are never free of the self, however much we would like to prove we are. Social inequity makes us uncomfortable. We harbor deep suspicions about the virtue of rich people if we are poor, of our own virtue if we are rich. If we are somewhere in between, we are likely to be uneasy and ambivalent or deeply entranced in denial.

In fact, there are two possible ways to produce and distribute goods and services—exploitive and symbiotic. Technologies and ingenuity can serve either mode. The first is based on scarcity egonomics, the second on abundance consciousness, which is about balance, not excess. The latter, however, requires a different mode of consciousness; it requires some level of self-awareness. In fact, ascending from the battleground of commodity fetishism—which is the confusion of body needs with our social-identity core need on the one hand, and the inappropriate identification of our sociability need with our need for cosmic grounding on the other hand—will not occur in any other way. Our society, having lost the ability to "speak relational," has grotesquely elaborated this confusion. Market capitalism as a dominant mode of production is based on ever-increasing markets (more and more people) for ever less rational goods and services. We are taught "body needs" of every description and learn to imagine that we were, indeed, "born to shop." We are not taught that we are what we want, because we do not trust our natural self or our desire nature—we do not trust love. Instead, we are taught that we are what we buy.

True Love Is the Answer

At some level of awareness, perhaps every day, we are aware of the hellish texture of scarcity egonomics. Part of us rebels at the certainty of death, the certainty that we are all alone, the cruelties of the war of all-against-all for survival. In Western culture, certainly in America, we have developed a compensating myth. Since that myth really is about who we are and what we actually want, it is pervasive, persistent, and ubiquitous. It is what an anthropologist might call our "romantic love complex"; it is our myth of true love.

Since there is no mystery more profound than love, almost anything we say about any form of it must be hedged about with uncertainty. We will explore what the Brenden Matrix may have to tell us about love's power and mystery in the next chapter, but for now, perhaps we can fairly state this principle of scarcity egonomics:

Love is a commodity.

Of course, this assertion is insane. And, to be sure, we do not normally think of our longing for romantic love in such cynical terms; we would prefer not to believe such a terrible thing. Yet simply consider the popular abhorrence of "free love" and ask yourself this: If love is not free, what should it cost? For all our well-intentioned homilies to selfless love, altruistic love, loving one's neighbor, our actual love strategies go awry. And among strategies that are often misdirected, the quest for romantic love employs many of them.

The most immediate and potent energy of loving in the human condition must be drawn from the natural self, from the magical child's sacred pentagram. Among humans, loving that nurtures is about intimacy, trust, and touch. ITT. We long for all the ITT we can get because at some level of awareness we know that is how we empower each other. If the world were mended, there would be a wide range of socially approved contexts for us to give ITT to each other. The consensus ideals of intimacy, trust, and touch (including sensual touch) would not be linked solely to special, "ritually purified" pair bonds. Special, enduring commitments would be honored, but so would a wide range of other sorts of ITT exchanges, all through the life cycle. Why would we accept what now we call "free love"? Because, finally, we would understand that if love is not free, it becomes a market commodity. We would understand that ITT exchange greatly multiplies the power of the natural self, reduces the power of the ego, and accelerates the journey to self-awareness. Of course, for all of this to make sense, our collective awareness would have to be different.

Out of the assumptions of scarcity egonomics, our core-need strategies for giving and receiving love must necessarily be short-circuited. We want ITT, but, all too often, we don't get it. Quite simply, we find it horribly difficult to let the natural self be natural when our daily lives are mainly guided by ego strategies.

The quest for romantic love proceeds out of the energy of the self. Falling in love is, in part, about the encounter of souls. But when we are operating from ego consciousness, I suspect all of this is often misunderstood. Not always. But very often.

The quest for that special other person who will fulfill us re-creates the myth of Theseus and the labyrinth. At the heart of the labyrinth is this paradox: out of self-consciousness, as opposed to ego consciousness, being in love is our natural or ground state. In the web of the relational order, in or out of time, the self is love. There is no place else we can actually be except in love. Therefore, to "fall in love" is to stumble briefly into our relational ground state. But then, because we live in bodies-in-time and see the world out of an illusion of the self, we must negotiate the labyrinth and avoid the Minotaur of the ego.

Among shadows in the maze that so often fall around people who would be lovers are Oedipal projections, the clash of ego ideals, resulting in inevitable "control issues" and other sorts of power games—sexuality conditioned by gender roles that are typically not the same for men and women—and the fear of inti-macy. It is the effort to manage all of these things that reduces Eros's enchantments to market negotiations, that pushes us toward the tedious business of treating love as an exchange com-modity.

We can summarize all of this mayhem fairly simply. We often spoil our love affairs because, out of scarcity egonomics, neither party actually feels deserving of love. That's the first problem. The typical strategy for managing this is a mutual presentation of a special "deserving" courtship persona—a special version of the ego ideal tailored for the beloved. Since the courtship per-sona is stressful to maintain (it is guilt-driven and inherently about insecurity), the spontaneous channel for giving and receiv-ing love is narrowed. It's hard to be spontaneous and playful when you are self-consciously "playing at" being spontaneous and playful. Out of the inevitable disillusion that follows, since we can only maintain these "fronts" for a little while, the affair ends or a "bargain" is negotiated. You "owe" me such and such carnal and emotional support, in exchange for which I will pay you such and such carnal and emotional support. As soon as these "bargains" are struck, the lovers have entered into "spouse" roles (whether or not they are "legally" married and even if they are of the same gender), which are, typically, more or less unconsciously entrained to their parents' roles. We tend to imitate our parents' ego strategies for projecting blame, making guilty, and so on. When we do this, a shroud is cast over the power of intimacy. The interface of the lovers' interactions becomes tacit expectation and accumulated blame.

To "fall in love" is actually to be "floated out" of ego consciousness by a collusion of the natural self and the shadow power of the ego—our inner "trickster." Even when the experience is one-sided, it is always a learning experience. It is a way for the higher self to spring us free of ego-level awareness for a giddy season, a way to reveal the boundary of our fragile illusions of control. Lovers may find the denouement of their affair painful and poignant, or they may, possibly, use the power of their brief transcendence to empower each other in a re-visioning of their world. That is, erotic love may lead us to the edge of ego awareness and beyond; it may actually shatter the boundaries of illusion. Sadly, though, Eros's gifts are more often reduced to the cheap tender of scarcity egonomics.

Behind the masks of illusion are the faces of innocence. But until we have faces, to borrow a phrase from Madeleine L'Engle, there is work to do. Among our joint tasks is the remembrance of what we will call the "relational imperative." Just what that is all about will engage us in the next chapter. Meanwhile, we can practice the magical arts of self-honesty, honor the three principles of consciousness transformation (even though we don't yet know quite what they mean), and we can

Just do ITT.

Intermezzo

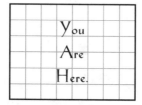

The next chapter is about love. While love is the broadest and deepest mystery, we have only two choices with respect to its powers. We may attempt to shield ourselves from them or we may permit them to flow through us. As *The Course in Miracles,* a remarkable manuscript "transmitted" through seven years of effort by a psychologist, Helen Schuctman, teaches that moment by moment, we choose love or fear. We cannot choose a little of each.

The choice between love and fear is made for us, collectively, by what in matrix theory is called the "psychosocial exclusion principle." Social worlds that devalue the relational mode of knowing choose fear. To choose fear is to enter onto paths of unconscious intentionality, to learn through pain instead of through joy. Fear is the hidden passport we carry in our soul's tour of dark enchantment.

The alternative to intentionality is intent. Intent is to waking as intentionality is to sleep.

Becoming aware of love present is the silent dawn of remembering that permits intent.

Intent is conscious choosing.

8

Choosing II: The Power Matrix

Love is anterior to life,
Posterior to death,
Initial of creation, and
the exponent of breath.

Emily Dickinson

We may say these things of love: It is the energy of Being. It is the binding energy of the cosmos. It is that which suffuses the hidden relational order and springs into the sensory realms in fountains of light as photons, electrons, atomic quanta, carbon molecules, or grandly rotating galaxies. The fabulous beauty and terror of the light and shadow carnival of a billion billion stars is a mask of God. A love mask. Your thoughts as you read these words are a mask too, a mask held by your intent. For as you choose meanings, consciously or unconsciously, you transform the beadwork of ineffable instants that are nothing less than your life unfolding.

Love is what appears and what may appear; it is a love letter dropped into a hearth fire with trembling fingers, and it is the pain and longing behind the words that turn to ashes. Love is the touching of hands in the entrancement of mutual discovery, the haunting of a poet's pen, children laughing in pursuit of fireflies. It is a shared sandwich in the gloom of a coal shaft, the passing of the Eucharistic chalice, the color of moonlight. Love is all of these things, but it is above and beyond what we may say of it. For, as we are a mystery to ourselves, so is love a mystery. And, certainly, the deepest mystery we may attempt to grasp is the mystic's insight, that what we are is love.

Even so, out of the intellectual model called "matrix theory" there is a clue. Imagine that for each of our core needs there is a tuning fork that vibrates sympathetically to the frequency appropriate to it. Now imagine a basic energy at the foundation of the cosmos. This energy is visible and invisible; it entangles what may be with what appears. It is what Plato intended by his concept of the Good; it is what mystics, sages, and poets may intend by the word "love." Now this ultimate substance of the universe-life-love-mind-energy expresses itself in every pitch, in every key, in every frequency imaginable, producing every harmony we can conceive of. Of course, this basic energy also permits every potential dissonance available out of the freedom of life's expressions. Freedom means splinters and accounting errors and sprained ankles. Yet please understand that this talk of frequencies is not metaphor or poetic license. Everything in the space-time realm, a benzene ring, an electron, or—taken as a gestalt—the billions of ordered peptide bars that create the latticework of DNA, have particular, empirically observable frequencies. Everything we call matter vibrates. When the matter is molecular, the vibrations are like those of chords. Just as there is a C-major chord, there is a silicon dioxide "chord." The frequency of a quartz crystal, stimulated by a tiny electric current, is what your digital watch "counts" to reckon time.

For humans living in bodies in time, there are four "primary love-life energy frequencies"—one for each core need. In the language of our tuning-fork metaphor, there is a correct "pitch" for each "core-need tuning fork."

Quite simply, the forms of love are the direct answers to our deepest questions and our most profound longings. Out of love's frequencies are the direct, wordless answers to the existential dilemmas posed by each of the four quadrants of the Brenden Matrix. Our need for cosmic grounding, our need to give and receive love, our need for social identity, and our need for bodily survival are answered directly and unequivocally by the forms of love appropriate to each need.

That is not a new idea. It is also not an idea that we can make sense of out of scarcity egonomics. The assumptions of the ego are about limitation, about the forms of insecurity and of fear, not love.

THE RELATIONAL IMPERATIVE

To know that only action out of love allows us to express our power and our identity is to rediscover a deep understanding, an understanding we have called the "relational imperative." If one was to ask for the simplest definition of this principle of natural ethics, it might be this: When the three laws of consciousness transformation—harmlessness, nonjudgment, and forgiveness—are apparent and self-explanatory, we have remembered.

In fact, though, that sort of awareness is not characteristic of ego-level consciousness. Ego dialogues, whether they are inner or outer, are about repudiation, self-justification, blaming.

For example, middle-class American children learn that it is not polite to attack one another. Don't hit; don't kick; don't bite. It's not nice. In fact, however, once primary socialization has helped us establish an ego, we operate out of ego dynamics. That is, we attack and defend. However, as we learn the principles of scarcity egonomics, we also learn to veil our attacks. Denial waxes and wanes in us as we do this. We have a need to feel that we are "good people," after all. We defend the ideal image we hold of ourselves, our ego ideal. Therefore, we learn to imagine that verbal and emotional ego strategies are not really attacks. You may not wield a kitchen knife at the throat of your mother-in-law perhaps, but you may feel perfectly justified in cataloging her errors, projecting blame, and perhaps stealing her life energy by making her feel guilty. In any case, we rationalize our attacks as "appropriate behavior," "just criticism," or something of the sort.

On remembering the relational imperative, we first encounter disillusion. The banal, shame- and guilt-laden cuts and barbs of friends and relatives begin to emerge into our awareness, not as exceptional incidents, but as tedious, vicious patterns. Worse, we learn that we play the same games, pursue the same kinds of ineffective ego strategies. We find ourselves busily adding our own toxic strands to a web of deceit that denies the web of connection.

When we are working toward self-knowing, pushing at the boundary of the consensus reality, it takes a while before we begin to grasp that any attack against another, any form of judgment, repudiation, or projection is, in fact, an attack against the self. Harbingers of the relational imperative arrive, however. They are built into us. The messengers may come in various ways out of objective and inner presence, out of paying attention, but always the message is the same. Everything, everywhere is interconnected.

You may begin to sense that you and your enemy really are connected in the same web of conscious existing. Or your messengers may come in some other form. You may begin to discover that you are not your body. Or, perhaps, through inner presence, you will begin to know that your awareness may move "ahead" in time. You may glimpse what is going to happen before it happens.

Attending to any of these messengers is sufficient to make us question the consensus reality. If something there is that doesn't love a wall (to steal a line from Robert Frost), we may then begin to question the value of the wall we have made between consciousness and its manifestations. Or, in terms of Brenden Matrix geometry, we may learn to question the boundary between the self and the not-self, between who we think we are and what we think the universe is. When you or I do that, we will begin to suspect that your consciousness and mine disturb or caress the strands of a cosmic web that is our common home. Your actions and mine, your thoughts and mine, are connected.

That is why I cannot attack you without attacking myself. The relational imperative begins to unfold in us when we begin to understand that this is so. But this realization will be wordless. It will be known, not supposed. When our actions are tuned to love's frequencies, they emerge from us as an impulse of intent, *not* of thought. Can you bring to mind how it feels when you are suddenly made angry? Pay attention to these moments. You will discover that you make a decision. The decision will be faster than your ability to think with words. In fact, the decision to express anger is about as fast as the way you incorporate the sound of an alarm clock into a dream. Never mind that you may then use thinking to rationalize your anger, to justify your projection. The decision comes first.

That which connects us to each other is not concepts or ideas or beliefs, but the quality of our consciousness. We act out of intent or out of intentionality. We express what we want or what we imagine we want. If we act out of intent we will not choose attack in any form, for that is not what we want when we allow ourselves to be guided by relational knowing. When we are tuned to fear and anger, on the other hand, our actions will express some shade or permutation of fear.

Intent is what happens when you are attuned to the flow of life-love energy. That flow is known through the relational mode of consciousness; it is not abstract and verbal. Most important, out of relational knowing we have options. Among these is the option to refuse tribute to shame and guilt. Selecting that option, intending it, we no longer need to face the world with hostility, for shame and guilt are always experienced at some level as an injustice done us.

Being free of the dynamics of anger and hatred, we will not court strategies of defense and attack. The self, free of guilt's frightful burdens, requires no defense. Finally, to make ourselves free of the need to attack and defend our precarious egos, we may choose not to honor fear. When we do this, we are made free of the need to cast the future into a shadowland of dread. A fear response is useful for getting out of the way of a speeding taxi. When a fear or "startle" response is not connected to an immediate body threat, it is nearly always projection. Projection is ego work. When our intent is tuned to love's frequencies, when we do not need fear, anger, or attack, we will not choose them.

Since we are mainly entranced in our moments of choosing, our actions flow less often out of intent than out of unconscious intentionality. If that were not the case, there would be no need for a book like this one. The power of intent only flows in the innocent tide of our desire nature, out of the magical essence of the natural self. Only as we are aware of what we want do we make authentic connections with ourselves and others that energize and transform. Actions that would restrict or redefine or limit the self are short-circuited and, ultimately, impotent. They are instructions we give ourselves about how to feel isolated and powerless.

THE WEB OF CONNECTION

Imagine energy flowing from the center of a complex, multidimensional web of connection throughout space-time as well as throughout the timeless relational order from which our matter-energy universe is born. If you like, imagine that the center, the Source from which all of these probable and manifest connections flow, may be named by any of the endless names of God. Action in the right "harmonic," the correct frequency, transports life-love-energy through the unfolding cosmic flower of possibilities, of potential expression. Action intended, consciously or unconsciously, to control, possess, or limit that energy flow acts like a resistor at best. At worst, negative action creates a temporary "dead spot" or "black space" in the web of connection.

Egos take in life energy but do not utilize it effectively. Ego energy—which is blocked life energy—can only dissipate away in guilt or shame, like a cup of tea getting cold because we forget to drink it. In the physical universe that sort of process is called entropy. It is what happens when energy drains away and is no longer usable. Energy in any form, including love energy, has to be used when it's "hot" and the time and place call for it. While some potential electrical energy may be stored in a battery, trying to store love is like trying to keep lightning in a bottle. Life-love-energy isn't meant to be stored, but to flow. Love that does not express the natural self moment by moment slips away from us. We lose the usefulness of the energy. The only way to have life energy in limitless abundance is to be "in the circuit," to be part of the flow of love, not a tiny dam trying to catch and keep your little part of it. To have love is to give it; to give love is to have it.

FOUR LOVES, FOUR NEEDS

The heart of all matrix sets we may propose out of Brenden's compass for choosing is that which nests four faces of love in human experience. C. S. Lewis, a Christian scholar and philosopher, named these four faces of love, drawing on traditional concepts from classical Greek thought.[1] Here we will reconsider Lewis's four loves and see how they are related to our core needs.

FIGURE 1: THE FOUR FORMS OF LOVE ASSOCIATED WITH THE FOUR CORE NEEDS

	Relational	Objective
Self	EROS Giving and Getting Love	FILIA Social Identity and Approval
Not-Self	AGAPE Need for Cosmic Grounding	STORGE Need for Body Nurturance

In Figure 1, we see the forms of love as a Brenden Matrix set. The figure also nests the core needs associated with each of the forms of love. Just as our core need to give and receive love is the heart of our soul nature, of the self, what we touch on here is at the heart of what we may learn from the Brenden Matrix.

THE RELATIONAL OR STRONG FORMS OF LOVE

Eros is what we associate with romantic and sexual love, but its dimensions are broader and deeper than that. Indeed, Eros is nothing less than our vital energy, and some of that energy is always present in the "objective" or quieter forms of love—filia and storge—the love of friends and the love of companions.

Eros's mysteries are tangled through virtually every important myth of Western culture. Aristophanes, a guest at Plato's famous "cocktail party," *The Symposium*, recounted a myth that abides perennially in our quest for soulmates. As this story has it, humans were once of three sexes: male-male, female-female, and male-female. These strange, two-headed, multilimbed creatures were so powerful (and undoubtedly so strange to behold) that they threatened the gods. The Olympian remedy was a decree that the creatures should be split in two. We have been seeking our "other halves" ever since.

Oedipus slays his father, beds his mother, and suffers the torments of the damned, overwhelmed by Aphrodite's indiscriminate powers. Freud wove that myth into psychoanalytic dogma, but it is also laced into our cultigens, our "cultural DNA." The current fervor to discover the demonic in each other through charges of child abuse is an odd re-emergence of this cultural theme.

Arthurian legends' star-crossed tale of Lancelot, the noble King Arthur, and their ultimate tragic fate in the power of Guinevere's "fatal attraction," is a story repeated again and again in popular culture. Similarly, the tales of Tristan and Isolde, Romeo and Juliet—wherein love threatens social convention and ends in tragedy for the lovers—persist, yea, even unto *West Side Story*.

In popular culture, romantic love is the substance without which few song lyrics would exist; romance novels are one of the few genre fiction categories that still constitute a mass market for aspiring writers. Song lyrics tell us about Eros's perplexities and pains, especially in their country-and-western guise, while romance novels typically "step down" the mythic proportions of Eros's merry storms. Hero and heroine in these tales must have their passion redeemed in a socially acceptable formula, which, among other things, calls for a happy ending. In this form, romantic love represents a myth of fulfillment within the context of our perplexed social world and its narrow preconceptions. The heroes of romance novels, for example, are often traditionally patriarchal in their behavior and attitudes, the heroines only sufficiently liberated to be acceptable to modern temperaments. In short, our popular tales of romance are often merely myths about a myth.

Still, whether in song lyrics, TV sitcoms, Hollywood films, or mainstream novels, romantic love remains one of Western culture's few sacred domains. The grail quest is forgotten, but not the star-crossed quest for unconditional love. Even in the 1990s, romantic love breaks boundaries, crosses social-class lines, shatters illusions, and often enough ends in disillusion.

In *agape*, Eros's ultimate source, love is stepped up to a higher frequency. Orgasm becomes a mere metaphor for something yet more ecstatic and transporting. Sometimes called "the love of God for man," agape is transcendent of the self, alien to the ego, and quite beyond our illusions of control. It arrives. Sometimes it arrives softly, like a summer breeze, sometimes without warning, like a thunderbolt. Always, like falling in love, it is transformative. Saul was struck blind on the road to Damascus and became Paul. Francis of Assisi gave up his social position and confronted both social convention and the complacencies of the medieval church with his message of harmlessness and gentle community.

While we may express agape's power in us through all the forms of love, including what may be called altruistic love—which is agape made evident—we cannot command it. It is the power of Creation itself and It commands us.

THE OBJECTIVE OR QUIET FORMS OF LOVE

Before we became more sensitive to the sexism built into language, *filia* was usually called brotherly love, but, in fact, it may be better understood as the love that makes one a brother or a sister—whether they are related to us or not. In fact, C. S. Lewis, following Aristotle, wrote of filial love in the noble tradition of friendship. Friends support each other, help each other to grow, are loyal to each other. In any case, filial love is not simply the love we are expected to extend to family members (whether we feel it or not). It is the authentic love of friends. It is also the spontaneous affection and sharing of playmates. In fact, when filial love is authentic and spontaneous, it always draws on the playfulness of the natural self.

Storge may be thought of as companionate love. It is the affection that binds the consciousness of soldiers sharing privation and danger, of neighbors at a barn raising, of women at a quilting bee, of companions in trout fishing. In general, storge is the quiet affection of people joined in meeting common needs for nurturance and survival—whatever the social framework.

Thinking of love as life energy, we can grasp that we need that energy at different "frequencies" for different aspects of our lives. Eros and agape, the relational forms of love, are love's strong forms because they are transformative. Falling in love and into enlightenment are powerful, life-changing experiences, and, in fact, the boundary between erotic ecstasy and mystical experience is thin. Either may be threatening to us or to the social order. Romeo and Juliet died together, victims of the mutual hatred of the Montagues and the Capulets. Gandhi was assassinated. Christ was crucified. And in every instance, the world was made different.

The objective faces of love, filia and storge, are "stepped down" to manageable frequencies and serve different purposes. They are necessary to the maintenance of social groups, especially to the maintenance of communal groups, whether these are based on affinity or blood ties. Put another way, the binding force of social worlds, of our daily relationships with each other, would be filia and storge if our awareness did not vibrate at the dull, slow frequencies of egos. Everyone here, sharing the strange journey through the "Earth school," is your companion, and many may wait to be joined with you in friendship.

We need to feed on all four faces of love because we have four core needs, four "existential realms," which are about different faces of our existing. The sort of life energy that flows into a well-prepared meal is not like the energy that flows into the effort to soothe the fears of a frightened child. The energy necessary to tending a vegetable garden is not like that necessary to the business of organizing a ceremonial. To be sure, in any actual human enterprise, all four forms of love may be needed. Therefore, the practical problem of loving is balance. We need to learn the arts of love at different frequencies, for the different purposes of our lives.

BARRIERS TO LOVE PRESENT

Traditional wisdom from all the great world religions—and particularly their mystical lore—teach us that love is abundant. Indeed, the insight of the mystics is that the Creation is the Creator's and that the Creator is love.

Love is everywhere.

So why are we so starved for it? If the life energy we need to sustain us is everywhere, why do we treat it like the painted sea of the ancient mariner and, too often, die of thirst?

Of course, from what we have already said, I can presume you will have jumped way ahead of these rhetorical questions. The association of the core needs and the forms of love in Figure 1 was not about a curious parallel. The geometry of the faces of love is also the geometry of our deepest longing.

If this is so, we need to begin to understand how all of the forces of delusion and illusion we have already discussed can be understood in terms of getting the life energy we need. I believe there are two parts to the answer. First, we have to be reasonably convinced that what we truly need to be alive to the self is love in all its forms. Next, we need some clues about how the self-ego split and other dilemmas of the human condition can be handled as we learn to perceive the sea of love around us.

COSMIC GROUNDING: IS THE UNIVERSE FRIENDLY?

Our need for cosmic grounding is not fulfilled by getting an intellectual insight, by joining a church, or even "getting saved." It is fulfilled in the direct experience that we are at home in the universe, properly connected at every point in the web of light, safe, fully supported, and unconditionally loved. That experience, in fact, is what is reported as the substance of enlightenment— to the extent that anything may be spoken of it.

Here is how the substance of enlightenment is expressed in the preface to *A Course in Miracles*.[2]

Nothing real can be threatened,
nothing unreal exists.
Herein lies the peace of God.

Here is how the same idea was expressed by Bernard Bosanquet:

And now we are saved absolutely, we need not say from what,
we are at home in the universe, and, in principle and in the
main, feeble and timid creatures as we are, there is nothing
anywhere within the world or without it that can make us
afraid.[3]

The answers to our cosmic questions are not available through concepts, myths, or theologies—although any of these may serve as guides. Certainly our deepest questions cannot be answered by classical science—even when that is a guide. When the answer comes, it is through immediate, undeniable, and concrete experience.

Will I Be Happy If I Find My One and Only?

Nothing is more compelling or confusing about life in a body on planet Earth than our sexuality. And nothing is more perplexing than the relationship between sexuality and love.

Eros is a face of our life energy; it is ubiquitous in human consciousness. It represents the face of desire and the pain of disillusion more immediately than any other area of our lives. I suspect that untangling the meaning of our sexual desiring and the compulsions of romantic love must reveal something very profound about our human nature and our human predicament. But I also suspect that the Gordian knot entangling Eros and Dionysus is beyond simple comprehension. That mystery is the mystery of human nature itself.

In Western thought, at least, people in search of things spiritual have been encouraged to deny the sensual in favor of things otherworldly. The sometimes explicit association of the ecstatic transport of lovers and the quality of the experience of enlightenment, when reported by Western mystics, has generally been kept out of sight and certainly out of cultural norms. To my knowledge, only in Taoist and Tantric teachings have sexual energies been attended to systematically as means to spiritual ends. Gandhi, for example, is reported to have slept sandwiched between young girls, not for carnal gratification, but simply to draw their feminine energy. It was a matter of Eros for health, not hedonism; it was about allowing a modest measure of sensual energy to flow through patriarchal cultural norms.

As a practical matter, if we are concerned with getting in touch with our core need for giving and receiving love, I feel that the Western spiritual tradition of sensual denial is not particularly useful. It may, in fact, be downright toxic. The peculiar association of sex and sin—a complex topic that is beyond the scope of this book—is, at least, *not* about self-awareness. Celibacy is only practical for a few. Efforts to make it normative, as in the medieval monasteries, seem to have met with mixed reviews at best. The historically recorded instances of abuses, lapses, and even orgiastic rebellions are informative.

Most importantly, the denial of natural sensuality is a broad highway into the confusion and pain of scarcity egonomics. The problem is about genitals. If the world were simple, pleasurable sensations associated with human genitals might simply be thought of as . . . pleasurable. In fact, though, it is seldom so simple. Most of us learn very early to associate genitals, along with anal and urinary functions, with the secrecy of bathrooms and forbidden feelings. That is, we learn to lie to others and to ourselves about what we feel. In effect, the pattern for normative lying and for self-deception generally begins with the shame and guilt associated with sexuality and, therefore, with sensuality in general. Lies and evasions about masturbation are like a template for learning to lie about everything else we feel. We learn that we masturbate, but do not masturbate, that we have sexual fantasies, but do not have sexual fantasies. We learn that there is a private self and a social self that must not touch. And soon we grow convinced that the private self, the place where we know our desire nature, is contaminated and must remain hidden—even from our own awareness. To be sure, through education, through resocialization into more permissive modes of thought, we may wear away some of the guilt and repression associated with our sexuality. But the template for evading inner presence, for inner lying, often remains.

To be sure, there is an antinomy here, a painful paradox. All social worlds have issues with genitals: the mutual stimulation of male and female genitals in proximity makes babies. Babies have to be nursed, nurtured, clothed, and fed. They also have to be named. In human social worlds, names are related to social rank, kinship groups, and social prerogatives. It is not surprising, therefore, that the pleasure of genital excitation furrows the brows of elders and generates a wide range of social complexes.

However, the design of a social world, the degree of its synergy—which is the degree to which any society provides knowledge of and access to effective core-need strategies—is inextricably related to whether or not sensuality is given its due and permitted acceptable avenues of expression. In Western culture, patriarchy has twisted our sensual and, therefore, our sexual nature into peculiar shapes. The meanings of genitals are hedged about with suspicion, shame, and guilt.

It is in this peculiar context that Western ideas of romantic love have developed. And the romantic-love formula, if there is such a thing, is incredibly messy. Here is the basic recipe: Mix guilty sensuality into a maelstrom of hormonal attraction. Blend in a poetic fury for explaining biochemicals at play (endorphin production, for example). Add generous measures of ego projection, ego strutting, and the emergence of repressed desire (often Oedipal). Force this mixture into confused and conflicted gender roles and simmer. The result, however elating, will probably be confusing and, often enough, painful.

Romantic love, I suspect, must be understood as the turbulent joining of at least three life-energy streams from very disparate sources.

1. Souls do seek to join souls. That is the substance behind breakfast at Tiffany's, singing in the rain, or being relieved of being sleepless in Seattle. And perhaps, honoring Aristophanes's myth, some souls do vibrate at complementary frequencies, so to speak, and, in the cosmic design, are more likely to fulfill each other. Perhaps there is some substance to the notion of soulmates. But the objective of the joining is the birth of a creature that is greater in power than either soul separately. In spiritual language, the goal is extension, for love's nature is the unfolding of what may be, of new possibilities.

But that is not what typically happens. We fall in love, yet we fail to become Aristophanes's glorious two-headed creature. We struggle with each other for control of the shared energy. As we have already noted in our discussion of scarcity egonomics, the end of the struggle too often is compromise, usually in the form of a dominance-submission scenario, or, simply, falling out of love.

2. The great subverter of the natural impulse of souls to join is egos. And the power that egos call on is that of the shadow. At the outset, on the tacit assumption that the natural self is suspect, the lovers are inclined to conceal it. In its place, each offers an idealized mask, a "courtship persona." These are ritually joined in honor of the mystery of two souls' encounter, no better ritual seeming appropriate. Instead of a double person we get two halves of personas. To patch up the "structural deficiency," we use the erotic power stored in the shadow to play sexual games, and when all else fails, to play make-guilty as a way of holding the "love" of the other. I suppose we do this because, ultimately, we feel safer hiding behind our masks than risking intimacy. We do not trust intimacy because we do not believe that what will be revealed deserves to be loved.

3. The consensus trance complicates matters further. Control dramas—like those inherent in gender roles—are socially endorsed. A way of managing the repression of the Oedipal content of attraction may be through honoring the parent by imitating his or her ego strategies—that is, control strategies. The most powerful role models we have for being wives or husbands are often our mothers or fathers, and we tend to imitate those models—even if we do so unconsciously.

In short, while we may not know how to manage Eros's energy for the transformation from codependence to superinterdependence, we sure know a lot about how to fall back onto our ego strategies. The magic of erotic love needs to carve out new channels for its energy. When that is made too difficult, the old familiar ego channels offer the path of least resistance, and the laser-beam coherence of the joined energies is dissipated.

The challenge of romantic love is the ascent to transcendence through intimacy. The goal of intimacy, always, is the rediscovery of the self through the clear channel of another's love. The end state, if it is reached, is the transformation of the lovers to a higher level of awareness through the power of their shared energy. The sharing of sexual pleasure can certainly be a means to that end, if its fullest value is not lost sight of. But, in fact, current cultural norms about physical ideals, sexual performance, multiple orgasms, and "scoring" are less than helpful in that regard.

The way from romantic love to the union of souls requires that the lovers give each other the heart and the courage to leap beyond the boundaries of the consensus world. Eros's gifts must be used for fresh vision and its power channeled into growing trust. Just as the mystery of enlightenment asks that one "die" in order to live—which, of course, is to die to the ego—lovers must die to what they were if they would be born into what they may become together. And in social worlds where individualism is a credo and a faith, where faiths have little substance, that does not happen much.

On the other hand, I believe, through patience, the channels of love and intimacy can be opened—even between people whose marriages have fossilized around recipes that all but exclude true intimacy. The love energy is always there if life partners have a mutual will to share it. The present is always present. Old control strategies can be recognized and undone; trust can be learned; the self in the other can be honored as we learn to honor it in ourselves.

LOVE AT STEPPED-DOWN FREQUENCIES

Filia fulfills community by transmuting social roles concerned with power into a symbiosis of social roles that empower. That is the crucial role of filial love.

Filial love allows us to play the hierarchical roles with more playfulness and less harm. If you are a teacher, a therapist, a foreman, a parent, even an army sergeant, you have options. You can subordinate others, robbing them of their power, or you may employ the frequencies of filial love to empower yourself and the people who are your role partners. Filial love allows social roles that are ranked to work together synergistically. For example, if you are a teacher, you may teach by superordination, thereby subordinating your student. That is how we teach each other powerlessness. That is also the way we imagine people should act toward one another in our social world. We have made hierarchies of social status, pyramids of power and privilege. Pyramids of despair.

If, for example, you are a teacher, and you would prefer to live in circles of hope rather than step over others in your climb to the top of your local status pyramid, you may empower yourself and your student by remembering always that you and your student are, in the relational order, equal creatures, equally created by the same timeless Source. The differences in time-space, in the cycles of growth, are temporary differences, not essential ones. Out of that frame of reference, you may know that all of the social roles you play are best understood as games. In our social world, we may play these games best if we remember that the outcome we seek is not power over another, but a common power, a new creation, generated by the game itself.

A good example of what is meant by the synergy of complementary roles is an orchestra. It is helpful in an orchestra for someone to conduct the different voices. Brass, strings, woodwinds, and percussion can best find their synergistic relationship if there is a conductor who is appointed to grasp an overall vision of the musical composition. On the other hand, a conductor without the power of the cellos and violins, the woodwinds and the brass, is a lonely figure waving a baton at shadows. Every part of the orchestra is a part of the whole. Every social role in a healthy social world is a part of a whole, part of a social game whose only ultimate utility is its realization of the core needs we all share.

We have the option of playing our parts in the daily dramas of our life as voluntary members of a social team. Perhaps, if we learned to grasp the subtle power of the Hopi insight, "cooperation without submission," we might learn to literally play our roles together instead of defending our status prerogatives. Life at work and in communities would have a very different quality.

There may always be a need for arranging roles in hierarchies of responsibility for certain purposes, but we can understand such relationships in different ways. Not as power games, but as a symbiosis of tasks directed at a shared goal, toward an outcome intended to benefit all the players.

Of course, recognizing the frequencies of filial love behind our hierarchical power games requires us to differentiate ego from self-consciousness. In his book *Exploring the Crack in the Cosmic Egg*, Joseph Chilton Pearce gives us the important insight that consciousness bound in linguistic conditioning proceeds through three "existential points," corresponding to our ideas of past, present, and future.[4] In fact, we referred to these three ego junctions above, in the Intermezzo. Out of ego consciousness the past is bound to guilt and shame, the present is devoted to hostility, the future to anxiety.

The alternative to this savage triad is found through tuning our awareness to the natural self and its timeless nature. That process is not easy, but it is the path away from ego compulsions, away from the need to disempower others by "ranking" one person over another. In the harmonic triad of the self, there is only love received, love given, and love anticipated. These are also the moments of the creative process—inception, extension, reception. We are inspired through insight and desire to produce a work of art. We extend that insight and desire into the object made manifest—the painting, the poem, the sonata. We then both receive the thing we have made manifest and offer it. The new manifestation may then flow inward, into our feelings and understandings, making our world richer and more interesting. However, such relational moments do not flow from past to future, for each relational moment is present in the other. Every relational moment, every facet of love's energy, turns in the spacious present, which is the only place we ever actually live.

We have not said much of storge in this discussion, although much might be said of it. Among those things is that companionate love is probably underrated. Many fine marriages have been more about companionship than passion. The essence of companionate love is honoring the instrumental roles of our companions, at work, at play, and especially in the demanding business of nurturing and caring for children. It is about fitting roles together. I measure so you may saw. I can wash while you dry. I'll try to keep the baby happy while you put on the diaper.

To live consciously is to live in the flow of relationships, to be in the web. We need to know that every tremor of that web, anywhere, everywhere, is a part of our transcendent connection. The sharing of instrumental roles, of simple tasks in a cooperative harmony, is a fine way to remember that. Every part of the web intersects where we are, right now. In that sense, doing the dishes is not all that different from signing a peace treaty.

Out of an awareness that is open to love present, we may affirm the bankruptcy of scarcity egonomics. We may recognize that the forms of love are the fulfillment of our core needs. They are what we want. What we want is who we are.

Therefore, to choose love is to choose the self.

INTERMEZZO

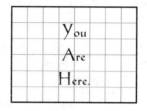

A sorcerer
lives through you.
A shaman dances in your
passing shadow,
magic flares from the crown
of your head and
trails from your fingertips.

There is no pain
no puzzle,
no hatred,
no fear,
that is stronger than your
innocence,
or impervious
to the passion
of Brenden's fire.

You need not believe this.
But you may,
when you are ready,
remember.

9

DOS* for Dummies

("Discovering Our Selves")*

They [Trudy's space chums] said,
"Trudy, we see now, intelligence is just the tip
of the iceberg. The more you know,
the less knowing the meaning of things means.
So forget the meaning of life."
I didn't tell them, of course,
I had.
See, it's not so much what we know,
but how we know, and what
it is about us that needs to know.

Jane Wagner, *The Search for Signs of Intelligent Life
in the Universe*

If we would move from the ego to the self, from what we think we want to what we need, we must follow our desire nature through the labyrinth of our life world, our personal experience, into the experience of the self. That is not a journey through space but, as *The Course in Miracles* reminds us, a journey without distance. It is a journey through consciousness states.

Although there are various metaphysical ideas about types and levels of consciousness—some of them very sophisticated—we probably cannot even imagine how many levels of consciousness there may be. For humans, certainly, there are a wide variety of what research psychologist Charles Tart calls "discrete consciousness states."

Gurdjieff, the great metaphysical teacher, instructed his student P. D. Ouspensky (a mathematician and mystic in his own right), that there are four levels of consciousness. The lowest level, he taught, is sleep. The second level is typical for us most of the time when we are in waking consciousness. It is a state of waking illusion. The third level, into which we may slip briefly, permits awareness of the self. The fourth level is full enlightenment.

TABLE I: CONSCIOUSNESS LEVELS

LEVEL I	Sleep States	Open Illusion
LEVEL II	Ordinary Waking States EGO-DOMINATED	Closed Illusion Reflexive, not choice ordered
LEVEL III	Self-awareness States SELF-INCLUSIVE *Choosing (alignment) is possible here.*	Dis-illusion and partial awakening
LEVEL IV	Transcendent States SELF-AT-HOME *Space-time carnival now optional.*	Awake Surprise!

Thinking about how our experience is related to different consciousness states can be very helpful. In particular, we learn that what we experience depends on our *focus state*, the "station" or consciousness level to which we are tuned.

LEVEL I

Within each level, a number of consciousness states are possible. In Level I, the spectrum ranges from drowsing, to ordinary REM (rapid eye movement) dreaming, to lucid dreaming (when we are awake in a dream state and the dreamscape is clear and detailed), to what may be called vision dreams. I refer to Level I as a domain of open illusion mainly because dreaming may allow us to escape the lockstep of conditioned perception.

It's a bit paradoxical, but we may be more "awake" to the powers of the self during sleep than while we are in Level II. You don't have to be a Jungian analyst to know that dreams often bring direct, relational messages. Scientists and artists often credit dream imagery for crucial insights. The starting point for René Descartes's philosophy was a dream or vision in which, all at once, he viewed "the order of the sciences." The German scientist Kekule dreamed an Ouriborus (a serpent with a tail in its mouth) and "saw" the closed carbon ring of the benzene molecule. Robert Louis Stevenson dreamed the plot for *Dr. Jekyll and Mr. Hyde*. The examples go on and on.

Dream states may lead us to self-awareness in other ways, too. People who catch themselves out-of-body for the first time may do so in a dream state. That was true for me. Robert Monroe, a bold pioneer in out-of-body exploration, is convinced that we can do a lot of important work toward self-awareness in sleep states.[1] And, if only because learning that we are not bodies is a big step in the quest for the self, I respect this judgment.

LEVEL II

Level II—ordinary waking consciousness—may also offer us assorted gates into altered states, some of which are more open than others. Practicing objective and inner presence or, simply, paying attention, is one of these gates, perhaps the simplest. Another, properly understood, may be trance work. Going into trance is not really all that mysterious; we do it all the time spontaneously. We become entranced while on a long drive, for example, or even in the middle of a boring conversation.

Moving into a trance state is not the same thing as dreaming, although there are similarities because of the alteration of our relationship to space-time, particularly in deep hypnotic trance. Light trance states are so common that most people are not aware of being in them. That is a fact that may have interesting implications for those of us in search of the boundaries of conditioned awareness. Indeed, it is one of the reasons I refer to collective social conditioning as a consensus trance.

In any case, it is easier for some of us to prepare for Level III awareness, to grasp synchronicities, alter manifestation patterns (change what you are experiencing), and do time-bending work (becoming aware of information that is not time-bound), out of altered Level II states because they are more open, less bound by conditioned perception. The routines that permit us to move to "alpha level," such as the Silva Mind Control system, auto-suggestion techniques, or imagery and affirmation work, while in a relaxed "border state," are all fruitful uses of light trance states accessible out of Level II.

LEVEL III AND BEYOND

Meditation states are a special case, mainly because they are not, in fact, consciousness states. Meditation is a way of being aware *in* a consciousness state. To be sure, some form of meditative practice is crucial to the quest for the self. That bothers some people. Our clock-driven, homogenized, prepackaged, media-lated world seems totally antithetical to what most of us think meditation is all about. We simply cannot imagine anyone who has to meet schedules and pay bills spending lots of time in the lotus position lost in beatific Mona Lisa smiles.

Fortunately, meditation is not what most of us think it is. To be sure, there are a wide variety of meditative techniques, and seeking out and experimenting with some of these is probably a sound idea for most of us. Since there are many fine guides to meditation practices, I won't try to discuss meditation techniques here. But I will offer some comments.

Meditation is not so much tuning to a particular level as it is a way of being focused at any level. Skilled meditators may remain in a meditation focus state while dreaming, while awake, or while at home—however briefly—in Level IV. For those of us who are not skilled meditators, it may be helpful to know that the practice of inner and outer presence, paying attention without judgment, *is* meditation. Surprise! And you thought you had to chant mantras or count your breaths. Meditation is, at its heart, a focus state that allows you to be tuned to the silent witness "behind your mind." Since meditative states and the simple grace of the natural self (curiosity, awareness of beauty, playfulness, sensuality, and spontaneity) are all aspects of our ground state, of the self when it is not encrypted in ego dynamics, there are an awful lot of ways to be "meditative." "Losing yourself" in a project, being at play on a tennis court, paying attention to the constellation of Orion on a winter night, making love consciously (as opposed to self-consciously), and simply being fully present (which is what spontaneity is all about) are all ways of meditating.

Meditation is not about getting to some mental place that no longer responds to the "chatter of our roof brain," to the cacophony of thinking. It is not an ascetic stoicism that patiently bears the clamor of the world without reacting to it. Meditation is remembering how to be who we are. It is the character of Level III consciousness. What we call meditation is the most graceful, efficient, and effortless way we can be who we are. Put another way, meditation is about re-discovering the ground state of our consciousness, nothing more. Nothing less.

The Level III states are where we may go to save ourselves, to save each other, and to heal the Earth. In fact, if we would rather be who we are than who we are not, Level III is the only place we can go. Level III is the way home; it is the threshold of Level IV and full awakening.

DIS-ILLUSION AND THE DRAGON

Meanwhile, Becky needs her diaper changed, Henry is late for his cello lesson, and the car insurance is due. Here we are in Level II, not really awake, not really at home, not quite sure what to do next.

Most of us have to work with Level II consciousness because that's mainly where we are. Then, as we begin to break into Level III, we have to deal with the shock of dis-illusion and with the dragon of the defensive ego.

Dis-illusion is a necessary discomfort when we begin to discover that who we think we are and what we think our world is about is illusion. Perhaps this phase doesn't have to be a long, somber dark night of the soul, but periods of sadness and pain are pretty much inevitable for most of us as we begin to become aware of the cruelties of ego dynamics and the sad vistas of Level II entrancement.

The dragon, on the other hand, is what the ego acts like when we begin to resist it, to withdraw from it. It will fight for its "life." You'll notice that when you start to make changes in your consciousness aimed at self-awareness. There will be times when everything will seem to obstruct your efforts to be nonjudgmental, for example. Efforts at self-honesty and inner presence—which may include some meditation practice—encounter endless distractions. You'll see—assuming you don't already know. I don't need to explain it.

Level III states are those marked by the qualities of the natural self: spontaneity, playfulness, curiosity, sensitivity to beauty, and natural sensuality. As far as I can tell, however, the first symptom of breaking out of Level II is the dawning awareness of what we have called the relational imperative.

The relational imperative does not suppose, it knows, that all things are connected, that I cannot attack another, or the Earth for that matter, without attacking myself, that reality is suffused with patterns of meaning, and that the patterns are leading us somewhere. In full awareness of the relational imperative, the three laws of consciousness transformation—harmlessness, nonjudgment, and forgiveness—become as obvious as a cup of tea, as simple as a smile. All of the great religious traditions teach the relational imperative in some form or another. However, as we noted in the preceding chapter, when it is assumed that it must be taught, it has been forgotten. One of our responsibilities while we are living in a body in time is to help each other remember. Whatever your unique life purpose, you can be pretty sure that's part of it.

The ultimate test for Level III consciousness is being open to Level IV. At that point we can assume we will have dropped all pretense of being unworthy and unlovable. However, since I'm a beginner, just learning to imagine remaining in orbit at Level III, you'll have to consult more advanced sources for getting some ideas about what Level IV is all about.[2] Consult them, but stay grounded in your own experience and do not fail to honor your self through self-honesty. I can only tell you that I have encountered the fleeting, simple certainty that Level IV is home. It's where we came from and where we eventually return.

LEAVING LEVEL II

If you are a budding bodhisattva or some other sort of spiritual or psychic adept, you may find the following discussion obvious. Sorry. It is written for us folks who are trying to balance critical thinking and new experiences of things unknowable and mysterious. Western culture doesn't do much to make us aware of the relational order that lies beyond the physical universe and is its matrix. It does even less to help us understand that spiritual matters are about practical techniques and actual experience that makes our life vital and meaningful. The fact that the New Age movement sometimes seems shrouded in noncritical dreaminess doesn't help matters much. On the other hand, traditional organized religion may create even more problems. It asks people to accept beliefs, that is, to enter into a reality-consensus contract, to accept creeds and dogmas. The problem is, beliefs are not in themselves particularly useful. They have to be filled with experience and insight or they are simply scaffolding around a building that doesn't exist. Asking people to swallow precepts before they learn how to deal with incepts doesn't encourage either self-honesty or direct, relational knowing. The idea is to keep perception open enough so that our tendency to get "hooked" on sensory input, to fall headlong into conditioned perception that traps us, is continually offset by inner knowing, by inception. That is the only way we humans will overcome the powerful tendency of social worlds to become too left-brained. That is what is necessary to overcome the psychosocial exclusion principle.

On the other hand, most of us wandering around in Level II trances, dragging along the baggage of Western left-braininess, need to start simple. And those of us who can't quite find what we want in conventional religion or religiosity aren't normally ready to start the quest for the self with our friendly local psychic or by picking up a few selected crystals from the local New Age store. So this is a short guide to Discovering Our Selves (DOS) for us left-brained dummies.

BOOTING UP OUR RELATIONAL SOFTWARE

Self-honesty and paying attention, the practice of objective and inner presence we discussed in Chapter 3, is the only place I know of to begin and begin and begin. Of course, something may happen in our lives to kick us in the pants, to force us, however briefly, to doubt who we think we are and to long for "something else." We may have a near-death experience, get divorced, lose a friend to cancer, face the fact that we are gay or lesbian and decide we have to deal with that. When these "reality alerts" go off around us, we may try to turn off the alarm and go back to sleep. Otherwise, we need to know where to begin making sense of our world. We may then choose self-honesty. We may then choose to pay attention.

Self-honesty is the "default" option for conscious choosing available to us when we are in Level II. It is our guide for learning how to move from scarcity egonomics to an awareness of the self. Learning to pay attention to what is around us, to witness our thoughts and feelings, to see what we want—without judgment—is the same thing as opening channels for relational information. Beginning to track the needs behind our wants is to step onto the narrow, winding road toward home. As we begin that journey, being aware of the four core needs and the three laws of consciousness transformation is important, even if we don't yet know what to do about them. They are basic "documentation" for our relational software. They remind us about what we are trying to do.

DESIRE TRACKING

Desire tracking, becoming conscious of what you want, is the only clue you have to who you are. It's that important. But since desire tracking is a novelty for most of us, it might be helpful to give some examples of what you can begin to explore through inner presence. Following is a list of questions. Don't work too hard at answering them. Witness your thoughts and your feelings. Observe without judgment. Or observe your judgments.

What makes you lovable? What makes you unlovable? Where do you think your hatred comes from? When you consider suicide, why? What message are you sending to yourself, to the person who might be hurt by your act? Do you want to die or just end your pain? (They are not the same thing.) In your sexual fantasies, what do you think gives you pleasure? What links the scenario to the sexual arousal and the orgasm? How do you reconcile your drive for sexual pleasure with emotional intent, with your feelings about love and nurturance? When you imagine someone has hurt you, where is the hurt located? What makes you think the person you are attacking isn't yourself? When you are sure you are alone, imagine another's aloneness. Where are these joined? Why do you think you are your body? Why do you think you are not your body? Consider every index of success and prestige that gives you a sense of self-worth. What makes you think any of these are worth anything?

Try to evade any implied answers to these rhetorical questions. No implication need apply. Think of the questions not as judgments but as Zen koans for your mind at play. If you don't like these questions, make up some of your own. When you get tired of inner-presence efforts, stop trying. Your relational mind will do most of the work for you anyway, probably when you are asleep. Remember, what you are looking for is an awareness of what you truly want.

You are what you want.

When you don't feel like practicing inner presence—although it may begin to happen spontaneously after you get in touch with the process—take a vacation through objective presence. Seeing, feeling the beauty of the quality of light on the front lawn, the warm water of the shower, feeling delight and amusement at the giggling of children with a secret is often the fastest and most direct way to boot up your relational software. It's also fun.

By the way, moments of inner and objective presence tend to be fleeting. They are sometimes as quick as the way you incorporate the sound of a phone ringing into your dream when you are on the boundary of sleep. Don't worry about that. Do honor those moments, though.

LEVEL II LIFE-WORK BASICS

The Brenden Matrix is a compass for choosing. That is, it is a guide to understanding, then to knowing that conscious choosing is about alignment. Choosing has no conflict in it. To choose is to know what you want and to choose it, not out of guilt or out of fear, but out of knowing.

Choosing is a tentative business at first. We get our thoughtfull plans confused with the guidance of intuition and feeling. As when getting familiar with new routines or new habits, it can be tricky getting used to the new focus state we are trying to adopt. Eventually, though, there will be some moments of choosing that are simple and effortless. You will know what you want. When that begins to happen you will be getting reinforcement from the web of synchronicities in which all of us live. That is, you will become aware of the pattern of your life. At that point, choosing may become playful, then joyous.

When at last we learn to live at Level III, choosing in full awareness, we may trust and know that we are acting in concert with a full, resounding earthy and angelic chorus of affirmation.

HEART WORK AND HANDIWORK

The heart of our desire nature is in our profound need to give and receive love in all its forms. That desire nature energizes and expresses itself in the qualities of the natural self. Now, recall that the expression axis in us flows from the natural self to the body self and back again.

In my view, the main lesson of that observation is that the proper role of the body is the expression of the natural self. Spontaneity, playfulness, curiosity, our sense of beauty, and our sensuality are fulfilled to the extent that the body becomes a vehicle for life energy, for love in all its forms. If such a situation were fully realized, of course, the ego would have lost its power. The mirror path between the natural self and the transcendent self would be clear, unclouded. Direct knowing, and genuine choosing, would become grounded in an awareness of the transcendent self. Indeed, in that condition, the transcendent self becomes the "guide" for the natural self just as it becomes the direct energizer of our actions with each other and with all life. Ordering becomes "cosmic entrainment." The sociable and the transcendent self work together, and illusions of the need for external agencies of force and control vanish.

FIGURE 1: THE EXPRESSION AXIS

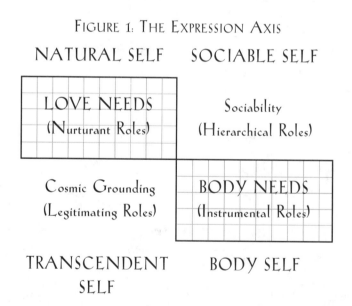

NATURAL SELF   SOCIABLE SELF

LOVE NEEDS
(Nurturant Roles)

Sociability
(Hierarchical Roles)

Cosmic Grounding
(Legitimating Roles)

BODY NEEDS
(Instrumental Roles)

TRANSCENDENT
SELF   BODY SELF

That's not where we are, though; it's where we are going. In the meantime, the Brenden Matrix has suggestions built into it.

Figure 1 is for thinking about the expression axis, the link between our heart nature and the body.

Here's a rule of thumb for handiwork and body work, for cooking and cleaning and exercising, for making pots and carving wood, for making art and paying bills. Be present in what you do. Let simple tasks be simple devotions. If you are working with someone, remember that storge, the energy of companionate love, is what fulfills the process of what you are doing together. That's practical Zen for dummies like you and me.

Intimacy: The Heart of Heart Work

Intimacy is about focusing on the love and nurturance end of the expression axis. Intimacy is being in self-awareness that seeks out, opens up to, or "entrains" (gets in step with) the life energy in another self. The way we do that is by allowing the natural self to express itself. That, of course, requires us to be in touch with our magical child in the first place. Intimacy is sharing our sense of beauty, our curiosity, our playfulness, our spontaneity, and our sensuality. It is not necessarily about sexual intimacy, although it certainly may be that. Intimacy is the meeting of children in trust.

When the way you use your body is not expressing the natural self, you are rejecting its only valid purpose and closing the gate on intimacy.

If another with whom you would share your self is closed to you, you must honor that. Share what it is possible to share. Or as a line from the play *Equus* puts it, "Worship all that you see and more will appear." To worship is to enter into shared presence. It is to know that you and I together, or you and the cosmos together, are more than either alone. To share even one dimension of the natural self with another is to allow a space for the others to follow, for they are, in fact, faces of one thing—Eros, our life energy.

ROLE WORK

Intimacy is the greatest gift we may share with each other. But there are many barriers to intimacy at Level II. Indeed, fully entranced people are not capable of intimacy, although they may receive love and healing (which are the same thing). As we begin to break into Level III, guidance as to how we may offer love and healing where it is needed becomes available. That guidance will come out of our intuition, especially as we become aware of the synchronicities patterning our lives. Inner guidance may also come as we learn to dialogue with our transcendent selves through prayer, meditation, or some form of "channeling." Meanwhile, when we must dwell in fields where intimacy is rare and precarious, balancing our core needs through our social roles becomes our daily work.

You will recall that each of the four kinds of roles may be played from ego awareness or from self-awareness. Through self-honesty, we can learn to witness the way we play our roles. As we do that, we may be able to undo the ego defenses associated with each type of role we are playing, and choose the better way. When we find we haven't the inner security, the cosmic grounding that allows us to surrender our defenses, we can still witness what we are doing with patience. And a sense of humor.

Table 2 summarizes the four role types, what they are for, their ego inversions, and the typical ego strategies associated with them.

You'll probably notice that a number of common social roles are missing. Some of these are aberrant Level II roles and not primary to the human core needs. A modern soldier or, too often, the modern police officer is first "devalued" (made powerless) through processes like basic training, then resocialized to adopt an altered ego ideal. The revised persona is designed to make the person an instrument of power for another's power strategies, such as those who monopolize the resources and wealth of nation states. To be sure, a soldier or a police officer can revise the demands of a social role for life-giving and empowering purposes. But that is not easy.

TABLE 2: THE FOUR ROLE TYPES: THEIR FULFILLMENT, THEIR INVERSION, AND EGO STRATEGIES TYPICAL OF THE INVERSIONS

ROLE TYPE	FULFILLMENT OR BETRAYAL
NURTURANT (Friend, mother, lover, healer, father, mentor)	Giving Life-Energy (Giving and receiving love)
Ego Inversion: Making dependent	Typical Ego Strategies: Making guilty, denial
HIERARCHICAL (Facilitator, administrator, coordinator)	Making a Place for Others (Giving social identity and approval)
Ego Inversion: Making powerless	Ego Strategies: Status-power games Being right, denial, rationalization
INSTRUMENTAL (Cooking, cleaning, making things, growing things)	Expressing the Natural Self (Symbiotic meeting of body needs)
Ego Inversion: Disrupting harmonies, ecologies	Ego Strategies: Making messes, destroying things
LEGITIMATING (Teacher, scientist, minister, scholar)	Empowerment of the Self (Cosmic grounding)
Ego Inversion: Making fearful	Ego Strategies: Projection, blaming, faultfinding

The modern soldier role should not be confused with the inner warrior role discussed by other writers. Inner role work is about expressing the power of the self.

Artist, writer, poet roles are aberrant in Level II Western social worlds. Just as every soul has an inner warrior, every self has inherent in it a natural artist, a creator that is, simply, an aspect of our magical child. That is, our inner poet-artist-writer-dramatist-dancer is simply the potential of the natural self. On the other hand, approved artist roles in modern social worlds are either artisan or craft roles or, too often, inflated ego (mask) roles reflecting the myths of a social world and, in general, misunderstood. Walt Whitman played social roles, for example. He was a journalist and a Civil War medic among other things. But, as a poet, he was a messenger from beyond the consensus trance. That's what artists do if they understand their calling. They may also bear terrible psychic wounds along with their gifts for us. Artists must cope with the problem of dis-illusion, which insight brings. Dis-illusion is what happens when we begin to break out of Level II but don't know how to stay at home in Level III.

Many other social roles in modern society are products of the psychosocial exclusion principle and the entrancement of ego-dominated Level II consciousness. They are *alienated* roles. They alienate us from our self-nature and our core needs. There are so many of these, mainly in the economic domain, from burger flipper, to textile worker, to many sorts of sales and clerical positions, I doubt that they need much discussion. Generally they are an effect of treating people like expendable machine parts ("task specialists") in production or distribution jobs linked to large corporate organizations. You don't have to read Franz Kafka or Marx or Max Weber to know that most bureaucratic and corporate jobs are alienating. In any case, you can tell if you are in an alienating role by how it feels to you as you begin to move toward self-knowledge.

That effort can be difficult since virtually all social roles, in all major institutional domains of our current society, are alienating in part. Education, organized religion, law, medicine, science, the nuclear family, all must deal with the paradoxes of the ego and the self. Our social worlds devalue relational-mode knowing and, therefore, the core needs for giving and receiving love and for cosmic grounding. We are out of balance, out of alignment, and don't know much about how to energize the roles, the sociable games, we play with each other.

DETOXIFYING YOUR ORDERING AXIS

Alienation is, at its core, self-forgetfulness. It is also the key problem for most of us living in our Level II–entranced world. It is the paradoxical conflict between living and making a living we mentioned in Chapter 1.

So what can we do?

Mainly, I believe, we can understand what the purpose of the ordering axis is in our lives. It is about meaningful action in the world, grounded in the security of knowing we are at home in the universe and safe.

The practical business of energizing our ordering axis centers on remembering that we can choose to play our hierarchical and our legitimating roles to empower ourselves and others. That is what I mean by "detoxifying" your ordering axis.

If you are a teacher, for example, you occupy both a hierarchical and a legitimating role. You have the option of exercising the power of these roles in service of the "self-esteem" demands of the ego ideal, or you can look for the ways and means that trade the "empty bowl" model of education for the "enfolded flower" model. Students are not empty vessels waiting to be filled with cognitive debris, with words and facts. Each student we are honored to serve is already a microcosm, full of intent and power. The relationship of student and teacher can be thought of as a dialogue designed for mutual growth. The end of "education" can be seen as one of awakening, of allowing the unfolding of the natural power of the self in both student and teacher, not simply as the reinforcement of cultural conditioning. That sort of idea used to be expressed in the idealism of teaching children "how to think." Perhaps, instead, we should be teaching each other how to know.

If your hierarchical role position is subordinate, as it is for many of us who work in large corporate or bureaucratic organizations, you may sometimes have the option of empowering your own role through a fresh vision of the tasks you perform. If you are a waitress, you can empower yourself by letting your role unfold as an expression of your natural self. Recall the Hopi principle "cooperation without submission" and wear your role lightly. In practical terms, that amounts to fulfilling Christ's instructions about walking the extra mile—but in your own shoes.

In any hierarchial role, whether it is superordinate or subordinate, in any job, you can explore ways to earn your daily bread and maintain your social place by embracing and fulfilling the tasks you are asked to perform. We can do that without expecting to be honored for it. For while we may, in fact, be rewarded for our affirming attitude by surprised and grateful bosses and supervisors, we may be resented by people who are threatened by anyone who operates out of their authentic power. Whatever the possible outcome, however, we do have the option of allowing the power of our grounding in the transcendent self to flow through anything we do.

FIGURE 2: THE ORDERING AXIS

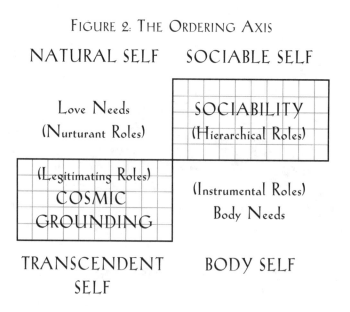

NATURAL SELF   SOCIABLE SELF

Love Needs   SOCIABILITY
(Nurturant Roles)   (Hierarchical Roles)

(Legitimating Roles)   (Instrumental Roles)
COSMIC   Body Needs
GROUNDING

TRANSCENDENT   BODY SELF
SELF

The ego, after all, is a no-thing. It has no substance in and of itself. It is a game we play; when we stop playing the game, we can choose another game or choose not to play games for a while. The ego is like the supposing that dances around in a ring; it is not the Secret that sits in the center and knows. Dream action has no real effects. When we wake up from a dream, we are still who we are. When we withdraw life energy from the ego, nothing real is lost, although we have freed up a lot of energy for life-giving purposes.

Most of us seem to have little choice about remaining in alienating social roles. But until we find the power of the self that allows us to make radical changes in our lives, we have the option of grasping the paradox and moving to a different frame of reference. We can do that through insight that grasps the principle of complementarity. Remember from Chapter 1 that complementarity is a principle of understanding that reconciles the irreconcilable opposites of our lives. In fact, the principle of complementarity in daily life is about seeing apparent opposites for what they are, which is, basically, an effect of a limited frame of reference. So, while you seem to need it, your ego is you and not-you. While we dwell in the dreamscapes of Level II, we are the roles we play and we are not the roles we play. That is the frame of reference out of which we can embrace the paradox, where we can begin to reconcile the cruel ironies of living and making a living.

While you are on the job, whatever the job, witness, do not judge. Re-form the role to your desire nature as well as you are able, but don't beat yourself up for not being able to undo petty office politics, the inhumanity of bureaucracies, or the wickedness of multinational corporations. When growing insight and synchronicities in your life guide you to it, drop a role that is too harmful, too alienating. Create a new role. You can do that when you begin to see that you are not the roles you play. We are not our dreams; we are the dreamers.

And that, gentle reader, after self-honesty and the three principles of consciousness transformation, is the main thing to remember. You are not your ego dreams; you are the dreamer.

INTERMEZZO

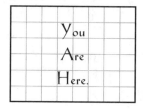

What seems to be the opposite of life is merely sleeping. When the mind elects to be what it is not, and to assume an alien power that it does not have, a foreign state it cannot enter, or a false condition not within its Source, it merely seems to go to sleep for a while. It dreams of time, an interval in which what seems to happen never has occurred, the changes wrought are substanceless, and all events are nowhere. When the mind awakes, it but continues as it always was.

A Course in Miracles: Workbook for Students

10

Immortality

It is an honorable thought
And makes one lift one's hat
As one met sudden gentlefolk
Upon a daily street,

That we've immortal place,
Though pyramids decay,
And kingdoms, like the orchard,
Flit russetly away.

Emily Dickinson, "Immortality"

The end and the beginning of your journey to the self turns on each moment of your intent, on each moment that aligns your desire to the self beyond the ego. We ascend or descend in the currents of our desiring, circling the timeless center at the core of our being. For we are that which desires, creates, extends, explores. Always we are nothing less than what we are; always we are nothing less than what we truly desire. To discover who we are is to know this.

We are what we are meant to be, yet to attend to our desire nature with self-honesty requires us to take a pledge of faith that what we want is good for us and for the Creation. Behind our pain and our confusion is the innocent power of the natural self. The Source of the natural self is our Creator. The nature of our Creator is love; therefore, that is our nature.

To know that these ancient messages are inscribed on our hearts may begin with remembering the relational imperative. That may be our threshold. But the pain of dis-illusion, which accompanies that remembering, forces us to turn into the shadow at the center of our fears, the shadow we call death. Re-visioning the meaning of death is the foundation of personal transformation.

THE DEATH ISN'T HYPOTHESIS

To learn again that what we are does not die is to begin to catch the light of the silent dawn into which all of us must, at last, awaken. Like the Lakota warrior who turns his pony into the face of his enemy with the cry "*Hoka hey* (today is a good day to die)," we must turn away from our clocks and schedules, our endless capacity for distraction, and look into the shadow of our deepest fear. It is a paradox. Only as we face the inner meaning of our death will we find the power of our life. The anchor of trust in the quest for who we are is a dawning realization that, as Phyllis Atwater puts it, "Death isn't; God is."[1]

Out of Level II consciousness the death-isn't hypothesis is not credible. Yet the way we see the world and each other is directly linked to our sense of death's meaning. If we imagine that our little lives flicker for a while in fields of matter, then go out, we are seeing ourselves as totally insignificant, as powerless, and as victims of an inexplicable cosmos. We also feel ultimately detached from the lives of others and either indifferent to the patterns and directions of our social worlds or compulsively engaged in reform movements that may be a substitute for actual cosmic grounding. (Altruistic work may be precisely what you will be led to, but it must be remembered that we cannot know how to fix social injustice or ease human suffering if we are out of touch with relational-mode insight. Without that knowing, we don't even know what needs fixing.)

On the other hand, just telling yourself that you will survive death isn't all that useful. To affirm a belief that is not grounded in direct experience at some level is only denial, simply an ego defense. Beyond denial, the quest for death's meaning may only be fulfilled in direct knowing. However, since there is within each of us that which already knows, which does not imagine we are simply bodies in time, the situation is not hopeless. While pursuing your quest for the knowing that does not suppose, there are tiny lights in the darkness you can examine. There are fireflies in the void of unknowing.

Among categories of "evidential" support for the death-isn't hypothesis, we may include near-death experiences, data suggestive of past-life recall, accounts of direct encounters with persons not in-physical, including the promising psychomanteum work of Raymond Moody, and out-of-body work, especially as conducted by associates of the Monroe Institute.

Moody's current research uses a mirror-gazing technique in a darkened room to permit persons to experience visions—sometimes of departed loved ones. It is interesting because it often gets results and, from a researcher's point of view, because it is easy to replicate.[2]

Monroe and his colleagues have explored the remarkable transtemporal geography accessible to persons who are consciously out of body. In my view, this work is chiefly of interest because it provides models for beginning to comprehend nonphysical, relational environments. What these explorers have learned also has powerful implications for understanding the nature of human mind consciousness.[3]

The research on past-life recall probably harbors the largest body of objective data suggestive of human transcendence. That is largely because of the meticulous work of Dr. Ian Stephenson of the University of Virginia. His work is painstakingly thorough and cross-cultural. As Stanislov Grof points out (see the article noted below), the data linking birthmarks in children to conscious recollection and documentation of apparent past-life trauma is the most remarkable body of this data and, from an analytical, objective point of view, the most difficult to ignore.

Of course, to all of the areas of inquiry mentioned above we must add the wisdom of the shamanic and mystical traditions, as well as a variety of "channeled" materials. Since this is not the place to appraise the latter body of writings—or their validity—I will not attempt to do so. I do, however, strongly recommend some of these works, including those "dictated" by the personality called Seth through medium Jane Roberts, and *A Course in Miracles,* scribed over a seven-year period by psychologist Helen Schuctman.[4]

In any case, we are brushing the hem of topics far beyond the scope of this book. The material supportive of human transcendence of mortality is so extensive and has been explored by so many writers that any review I could offer here would be hopelessly inadequate. For a summary of the situation, I recommend Michael Grosso's article, "The Status of Survival Research: Evidence, Problems, Paradigms," in the Winter 1994 issue of *Noetic Sciences Review,* as well as Stanislov Grof's article "Alternative Cosmologies and Altered States," in the same issue. You might also want to consult the works of Kenneth Ring, Raymond Moody, and Phyllis Atwater.[5]

Here I'll only offer some comments about one category of information bearing on the death-isn't hypothesis—near-death experiences. I do this partly to introduce the topic to people who may not realize how much data there is in this area, partly to make a few points about all of the information supportive of the death-isn't hypothesis, and partly because of my familiarity with this area of research. One of my doctoral colleagues, John Audette, was the first administrator of the International Association for Near Death Studies (IANDS). I've been following their work since the late 1970s.

NEAR-DEATH EXPERIENCES

Near-death experiences (NDEs) have become amazingly common in the last decades, apparently as a result of medical technology. Psychologist Kenneth Ring, who took the point position in IANDS research early on, has been one of the most persistent and thorough investigators of NDE phenomena. He and his associates have accumulated data on thousands of people, mostly in the United States, who have been clinically dead and have come back to tell interesting tales. What makes these tales attractive to the researcher who would dare the censure of fellow scientists is a convergence of characteristics. That is, NDEs have a typical form for people from very different social and religious backgrounds and even, apparently, from radically different cultures.

The typical NDE experience may begin with detachment from the body and a sense of peace and calm. The body is viewed from a distance; vision and hearing are not only unimpaired, but more acute. Conversations and details of procedure, in an emergency room, for example, are witnessed with a measure of bemused detachment. There may follow a sound, like rushing wind, or an unpleasant buzzing noise, followed by a "change of scenery." The experiencer may follow a tunnel outward, upward, toward light. At the end of this metaphoric or literal "womb," there may be loved ones no longer in-physical, guides, or, often, a luminescent and transcendent being, a being of light. These "light beings," sometimes interpreted as angels, sometimes as the person of Jesus (if the experiencer has been influenced by

Christian teachings), radiate loving power, which is at once awesome, unconditional, and reassuring beyond explanation or description. In the context of this sort of environment, the experiencer may be led through a life review or be admitted to a wide variety of metaphysical understandings.

Sometimes these understandings have included prognostications for humankind's future, which are also interesting in their common themes. Frightening scenarios related to our collective abuse of Earth's biosphere are not unusual, and they are often strikingly similar. Although the decision to return may be made by the individual, the return to the body is more often "involuntary." In either case, it is typically reluctant.

Interestingly, the cause of clinical death—pulmonary failure due to pneumonia, auto accident, or even attempted suicide—appears to have little bearing on the pattern of what Ring calls the "core NDE experience." Nor does age seem to be a critical factor. Children's NDEs are not much different from those of adults. And, as accumulating information is making more and more evident, near-death experiences are often profoundly transformative. Survivors often return with a passion for spiritual growth. They may also find themselves psychically sensitive or, in some cases, gifted with healing abilities beyond the reckoning of our consensus reality. In my view, these kinds of effects on NDE survivors have been most compellingly studied by Phyllis Atwater, herself a near-death survivor.[6]

It is important to understand that NDEs are very well documented. Beginning with the pioneering studies of Elisabeth Kübler-Ross, Raymond Moody, and Michael Sabom, through the extensive data accumulation by IANDS, there are now thousands of well-documented cases on file. Furthermore, that number accounts only for cases known to direct interviewers. A study by the Gallup organization suggests that the number of NDE cases in the United States alone is around 8 million. That's 8 million give or take a margin of error of about 500,000.[7]

NDEs are not oddities. They are authentic, concrete experiences that have touched the lives of large numbers of people. The manner in which the experiences may be interpreted is certainly open to question. But that the experiences are real for the subjects, often with astonishing effects on their lives, is beyond doubt.

When I put on my sociologist hat, I will readily admit that it is nearly impossible to research NDEs in the manner that the current scientific canon requires. In general, scientific proof, as we presently conceive it, requires variables that can be measured directly or indirectly by sensory observation, a logically satisfactory way of relating the variables under objective empirical examination, and a research design that can be replicated by other researchers. In short, inner experiences of all kinds, including consciousness states and our sense of the meanings of our lives, are excluded at the outset of scientific inquiry.

Among the paradoxes of our existence is this: At present, science is thought to endorse a particular world view, one that includes the assumptions of materialism, objectivism, and determinism considered earlier as Newton's triangle. Yet these "thoughts with which we think" are principles of scarcity egonomics and not, by any necessary logic, principles of science. Indeed, it is science itself—through relativity, quantum physics, systems thinking, and chaos theory—that has popped the Newtonian assumptions like so many cheap balloons.

Science operates in the cage formed by Newton's triangle. But that's only part of the problem. Scientists live in the same consensus trance as the rest of us. And, quite simply, "proof" of the transcendence of death out of the assumptions underlying the ego is a contradiction in terms. Out of scarcity egonomics, such an effort is a small, pointless journey around a circumscribed track in a field of illusion.

Dr. Larry Dossey has given us a succinct example of the way in which scarcity egonomics strangles the mythos of open-minded inquiry within science itself.[8]

Cardiologist Randolph Byrd conducted a 10-month study of 393 patients admitted to a coronary care unit at San Francisco General Hospital. Patients were randomly assigned to an experimental or a control group. As opposed to the 201 people in the control group, the 192 patients in the experimental group had their names given to several intercessory prayer groups from different Christian denominations around the United States. The members of a prayer group were given a patient's name and some information about his or her condition, and were simply asked to pray once a day for the person named. As it worked out, the patients in the experimental group had about five people praying for each of them over a day's time. The study was double blind. That is, neither the physicians on the unit nor the nurses knew whether a patient had been assigned to the "treatment" or the control group.

The following results were observed:

TABLE 1: SUMMARY OF RESULTS: CARDIAC CARE UNIT STUDY

	EXPERIMENTAL GROUP (192)	CONTROL GROUP (201)
Required antibiotics	3	16
Required endotracheal intubation	0	12
Developed pulmonary edema	6	18

All of these differences are statistically significant. That is, they are extremely unlikely to have been the result of random fluctuation. Fewer of the patients in the experimental group died, by the way, although that difference was not statistically significant.

In the cardiac unit study, we do not find sloppy science, we find an independent variable (presence or absence of intercessory prayer) that cannot be comprehended in the narrow field inscribed by Newton's triangle. As Dossey has pointed out, if these results had involved some new drug, the rush of the new pharmaceutical into the hands of physicians, complete with glossy brochures and free samples, would be proceeding at fever-ish velocities. The problem is not an absence of empirical information in the cardiac unit study; the problem is an absence of socially endorsed models for dealing with the information. The problem is not a bad research design; it is what sociologists attempt to explain to students in introductory sociology classes; it is ethnocentrism.

Beyond the demise of materialism out of respectable scientific models—like those of relativity, quantum mechanics, and chaos theory—actual research has accumulated genuine bodies of very real information about actual phenomena, about actual human experiences, which currently have no place in established science.

What may be understood by thoughtful people is that NDEs, out-of-body experiences, past-life recall, or nonverbal communication out-of-time are no more about illusory experience than are inquiries into the molecular structure of DNA or the mating habits of gypsy moths. It is our shared consensus trance, not the validity or rigor of the observations, that casts doubt on reasoned inquiries into telepathy, paranormal healing, near-death experiences, synchronicity, and related phenomena. Scientists, like the rest of us, are caught in the vice of the psychosocial exclusion principle and must wander about in the labyrinth of scarcity ego-nomics.

For you or me, the decision to use what is useful from these inquiries, therefore, must be based on a personal decision to "seek the truth, come whence it may, come how it might."[9] You will also have to get used to the idea that out of Level II consciousness no general consensus on the acceptability of these inquiries can or ever will be reached. For example, the reality of telepathy is the experience of it, not some objective measure of the phenomena agreed on by researchers. Making sense of such experiences is simply beyond conventional science because genuine knowing must call on all four psychic functions and on the complementarity of both modes of knowing. Don't expect to hear a CBS news broadcast announcing that authorities in some academic discipline or another have concluded that there is "life after death." Forget it. None of the phenomena that violate the principles of Newton's triangle or of scarcity egonomics will ever be acceptable to classical science. Science itself may, indeed, operate beyond the exclusion principle and the tacit materialist assumptions that entrance Western social worlds. But that sort of transformation in science will arise only as social worlds are themselves transformed through changes in our collective consciousness. Near-death experiences are not valid out of Level II consciousness; they are valid and meaningful as we move into self-awareness, however. And at that point the very meaning of "proof" is also transformed.

My suggestion is that as you begin the quest for the self you entertain these ideas: You will not die. You will not die because you are not your body. You—whoever you are—were present in the relational order before you got into this mess, and you'll still be you when you either get a vacation from the great space-time carnival or graduate. You are here for a reason, you will leave for a reason, there is even a reason you can't remember the reason. Yes, you will leave your physical body. (But you probably did that last night or the night before.)

To be in a body in time is to enter into a season, to take part in a particular drama among possible dramas spread across a panorama of such productions in what we call space-time. A body is the costume you use for your role. When your part is finished you exit, stage left. The curtain closes, you remove your makeup and enjoy a celestial cast party somewhere. Cheers.

Of course death is serious. It is the Great Seriousness of Level

II consciousness. Indeed, it is its basic rhythm. And that is the point. We cannot begin to conceive of ourselves or of others as bound in a web of love while our actual lives honor a half-buried faith in fear and death. While we are caught up in scarcity ego-nomics, the expression "God is love" is meaningless at best, a cruel joke at worst.

Just as we may begin to learn that we are not egos, we may begin to grasp that we are not bodies, either. These sorts of insights happen automatically in the quest for the self. So pay attention. Resurrection happens. In fact, it is inevitable.

In any case, while allowing yourself to be open to personal grounding in the death-isn't hypothesis, there are some other spiritual basics to attend to. Mainly they have to do with learn-ing that we have a spiritual dimension. Getting in touch with that, which is beginning to move toward Level III, is what we will consider next.

INTERMEZZO

Personal transformation is a journey, not a place at which we arrive. Love does not have a stopping place, only resting places.

In these pages we have considered our joint task in a time when the Earth groans and shudders with the pain of our collective entrancement. Salvation may be awakening, one by one, two by two, but the journey home must link all of us. Each of us. Everywhere.

The tools of transformation are as simple as a smile, and, in the face of our pain and confusion, as paradoxical. We must learn self-honesty, which is paying attention to our actual experience through both objective and inner presence. In this way, we may learn to trust and receive our desire nature, to accept the sacred pentagram of the natural self. This is how we learn to draw on our spontaneity, curiosity, playfulness, sensuality, and sensitivity to beauty. This is how we learn to know what we want and, therefore, who we are. In that unfolding, we discover our authentic power and the power of intimacy, which is the sharing of the natural self.

At the foundation of this alchemy of joy is a dawning awareness of our spiritual and transcendent nature. For none of these ways of seeking will bear fruit unless we allow ourselves to rediscover the relational imperative. To do that is to accept our place in the web of life-love energy that connects each of us to our Source. To find our cosmic ground is to become a channel for the healing power of nonjudgment, harmlessness, and forgiveness.

That is the simple topography of personal transformation. Expressed in the concert of dawning connections between us, it will provide the forms for social worlds that are both gentler and more challenging than those that are guided by the ego's cozy lies. The antithesis of this topography is the entrancement of our social worlds, especially as we devalue relational-mode knowing. Denial of the relational order draws us away from our core need for giving and receiving love. Lost to love's power, we forget our timeless place in the web of Being.

Beyond the dark litanies of scarcity egonomics, the principles of personal transformation and the model I call the Brenden Matrix provide a map and a compass. They are guides out of the long night of entrancement into our silent dawn. Beyond the mere topography of these words and ideas, in each of us the healing and the miracle are beyond reckoning, beyond words, and beyond measure.

11

Silent Dawn

Will there really be a morning?
Is there such a thing as day?
Could I see it from the mountains
If I were as tall as they?

Has it feet like water lilies?
Has it feathers like a bird?
Is it brought from famous countries
Of which I have never heard?

                    Emily Dickinson

The main barriers to ego evasion and the quest for the self are the aroused dragon of the ego's resistance and the despair we may encounter in dis-illusion. We may, for a while, be more conscious of our old world's dying than of a new one's being born in us and around us.

The techniques for dealing with the ego-as-dragon and with dis-illusion will vary for each of us, I think, but these are Level II consciousness properties, after all, and there are some guidelines for breaking out of Level II.

LIVING WITH DIS-ILLUSION

Life in a body in time is not a cosmic picnic. There is probably profound wisdom in the idea that our lives are initiations of a sort; the "Earth School" forces us to learn very hard lessons. The Buddha's first observation on enlightenment beneath the bo tree was succinct: Life is suffering. Perhaps, as Robert Monroe instructs us out of his explorations, graduation from this school is coveted by the mind-energy creatures who become entranced by this blue orb in the edge of a particular galaxy. A karmic tour of the great space-time carnival may produce magnificent creatures. But while we are here, with our credit cards and our Maalox, with our consciousness pulled into a lacework of disconnection by the random thumping of car stereos, TV sitcoms, and a million million messages about what we must buy to make our lives all better, it is hard to know that.

On this side of what the Greeks called *lethe*, the "veil of forgetting," there is horror mixed in with the boredom, irony threaded like psychic fractures around moments of wonder. While we are tuned to the collective Level II broadcast, death seems to define life.

On the other hand, if there is a difference between the ego and the self, between what we imagine ourselves to be and what we were created to fulfill, we can learn the twin lessons of the Earth School. First, we are responsible for what we experience. Second, we can choose love over fear, joy over pain. What we see out of Level II consciousness is what we get when we are tuned to the monotonous drone of scarcity egonomics. What we learn to expect pours into our awareness as manifestation. Our power to manifest the effects we experience is that great and that foolishly employed. Perhaps, as we learn from the sages and mystics, the effects of these manifestations are, ultimately, meaningless— not illusion in the sense that they do not have existence, illusion in the sense that a slide projection of an image requires us to consider the mechanism of projection (mind consciousness) and the underlying intent that selects the image.

DISARMING THE EGO

Persistence and patience are spiritual virtues, so be patient and persistent as you begin to question the reality of your ego. When, as it will, your ego self rises as a fire-breathing dragon, alarmed at your presumptuous efforts to tempt its vicious prerogatives, remember that it is your dragon. Be as patient with it as you can. Treat it like a kitten that insists on jumping into every door you open (like the idea that you are not your body), that tips over your wastebasket (dumping fresh guilt all over your clean ego ideal), that climbs the screen in pursuit of a moth at two in the morning (just when you're sure that what you really need is sleep). It's your dragon after all, your ego guardian. It thinks it's supposed to guard the treasure you've allowed it to spirit away into the dank and frightful cavern you may think of as your unconscious. Also, it's frightened that you will abandon it.

You will not abandon it. You will, in time or out of time, learn to talk to it until, when it is sleeping, you will unimagine it.

DISCOVERING YOUR FOURTH DIMENSION

If you've ever experimented with hypnosis, you may have discovered an odd thing. Hypnotic trances are not all that mysterious. We slip in and out of what we call trance states all the time. The persistent clack of a windshield wiper on a long drive can do it. For that matter, just driving over a familiar route can do it. (Have you ever been driving along and discovered that several miles have passed when you weren't paying attention? Bingo.) When people are first hypnotized, they typically are sure they are not—

until, for example, at a suggestion, their hands float up from their laps. The ordinariness of what hypnosis feels like comes from a simple fact. Nearly anyone (probably everyone) can access that consciousness state. It's part of our human repertoire of consciousness states; it's not a big deal.

Your spiritual dimension is a bit like a trance state in this sense: it is always there. Discovering your spiritual dimension is a bit like discovering you have a nose when you are three years old. (Oh, I have a nose.) Don't expect cosmic alarms and metaphysical fireworks. Your spiritual dimension is the framework of your awareness and your existence. It is also an immediate aspect of your consciousness, right now. Becoming aware of that fact does not require a course in metaphysics or eighteen years of contemplative prayer.

In practical terms, there are at least three ways to become aware of your fourth, cosmic, dimension, your transcendent self. These include becoming aware of your silent witness, paying attention to how your dreams work, and honoring moments of unaccountable joy.

Your Silent Witness

Paying attention through inner and objective presence is your immediate passport to your silent witness. Recognizing that there is that in you which is not your mind, not your body, not your emotions, is a giant step in the quest for the self. That witness, not bound by space or time is, quite simply, the immediate face of your transcendent self.

Discover Your Dream Producer

In paying attention to Level I consciousness, to your dream states, you may become aware that, while you are dreaming, there are three frames of reference—plus one. First, you experience the dream action; you are "in the dream." This actor frame of reference consists of a "subject" and an "object" aspect, rather like the feeling-to-sensation or the love-needs-to-body-needs axis of any matrix set. The "action" part of a dream is its "expression axis." The axis joins what is happening in your dream to your feeling experience of it.

But we also "watch" the dream as an observer. The observer part of dreaming is the equivalent of the ordering axis of any matrix set. In this case, it has a grounding part and an interpreting part. We both "think" about a dream in progress, converting imagery into word symbols, and we *produce* the dream. Exploring your "dream producer" is a way of finding your fourth dimension. Consider the following matrix set.

FIGURE 1: A BRENDEN MATRIX SET: FOUR ASPECTS
OF DREAM CONSCIOUSNESS

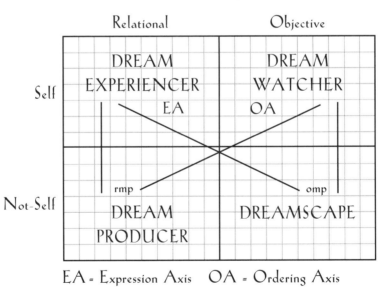

EA = Expression Axis   OA = Ordering Axis
rmp = Relational Mirror Path
omp = Objective Mirror Path

Looking at Figure 1 you can see that the *expression axis* (the diagonal from upper left to lower right marked "EA" in the figure) links the dream experiencer and the dreamscape. The Dream Experiencer is *you* as you feel fear, desire, nostalgia, revulsion, surprise . . . at whatever you find in the dreamscape. And paying attention through inner presence on waking from a dream helps you see what this expression axis link is all about. What we dream is a wish at some level; it is a projection out of feeling or desiring. But remember, since the upper left quadrant of the Brenden Matrix represents the "heart" of us, it also represents the pentagram of the natural self. Dreamscapes are playful, exploratory, sensual, astonishingly spontaneous, and always "colored" by the aesthetic qualities of love (which is desire in alignment with the true self) or fear (which is desire misplaced out of ego dynamics). That is, what's lovely in a dream is about love; what is ugly is about what we fear.

The *relational mirror path* (marked "RMP" in the figure) helps us see that our heart-and-soul state while we dream mirrors our cosmic grounding state. Your dreams will change, their content and quality will be different, as you push away from Level II consciousness into Level III.

The ordering axis in this matrix set (marked "OA") links the Dream Watcher–Interpreter and the Dream Producer. To the extent that you can consciously enter into the Dream Watcher quadrant, making that your primary focus state, you can order and manipulate your dream state. In full bloom, this sort of Level I awareness is called lucid dreaming. You are in a lucid dream when you are aware that you are dreaming and capable of ordering the dreamscape. Among the Senoi of Malaysia, where dream work is taken very seriously, people learn both how to interpret and how to order their dream imagery.[1]

Opening your awareness to the not-self domain of the fourth quadrant, to the domain of the Dream Producer, is to become aware of your transcendent self. To do this is to move from dreams that "just happen to us" into the realm of intent. It is possible to do this in a lucid dream. When, or if, you manage this, you will discover that your intent operates at a level that transcends the simpler business of "watching" your dream. You will touch the part of you that knows and guides the patterns of your life.

The mirror path between the Dream Watcher and the Dreamscape changes as you become more aware of and grounded in your transcendent self. Your dreaming reflects what you are open to as an observer and interpreter of your psychic landscape. When we are honored by the transcendent, fourth dimension in us, our dreams may become visions and guides. But that happens mainly when we are ready to honor the dream producer that is beyond dreaming—our spiritual dimension.

GROUND-STATE AWARENESS

The happiest way of knowing your transcendent self is through honoring moments of quiet peace and joy. Such moments happen spontaneously for all of us from time to time, but they can be courted. Paying attention, desire tracking, and a commitment to the quest for the self bring these instants of light and knowing into our awareness more frequently. Here is an exercise that may help.

Allow your mind to hold the image of a beautiful, innocent, happy child standing in gentle sunlight in a field of wildflowers. Imagine the child's core needs being evident, pristine, and undistorted, each in perfect balance with the others. Pretend that this child, in harmony with self and cosmos, with a graceful body and a delighted, curious mind, full of playfulness, laughter, and the creative power of Eros (life energy), is you. Because it *is* you in your ground state, at home in the universe. This is your natural self.

In this ground state, sensation is a medium, a stimulus language of the yin and yang of feeling, of being-in-relationship. The body is a vehicle for giving (yang) and receiving (yin) the energies of relationship in which we find who we are. In this amazing condition, the ground state of thinking may be called by the term "wisdom." Wisdom is what happens when our transcendent psychic function-intuition informs our thoughts. In our ground state, thinking explores the possibilities of the cosmos out of intuition, out of direct knowing that requires no explanations.

As you begin to have little breakthroughs out of Level II, moments of stillness, of unaccountable joy, honor them. Count them as "angel feathers." Store them in your heart for quick availability when you need an angel feather—like the next time you are tempted to hate someone who holds a point of view you despise.

Moments of unconditional joy do happen. When they do, it is important to recognize that they are not contingent on what is happening around you. Beyond the shadows of scarcity egonomics, peace and joy are your inheritance.

LOOKING FOR LEVEL III

While working with the death-isn't hypothesis and becoming aware of your transcendent self, odd things may begin to happen. You may become aware of dimensions of your mind consciousness that you were not aware of before. Honor what you are experiencing. Forbid the ego its fierce need to convince you that anything and everything may be real except your immediate, actual inner experience.

TIME BENDING

By becoming aware of the thoughts that pop into your head, which is part of paying attention, of inner presence, you may begin to discover that some of your unexpected thoughts precede an event. You are "time bending." (The common denominator of all sorts of psychic or paranormal communication or action— telepathy, clairvoyance, telekinesis, and so on—is "time bending."

The apparent limits of space-time are, however briefly, transcended.) Recently, for example, I attended a meeting of people at work finding new ways of relating to each other and exploring the meaning of community. Arriving back at my apartment, I thought of a friend who lives in a distant city, wondering what she might think of these bright and sensitive people. She is a once-a-year long-letter friend. Checking my phone messages, I found there was only one. From her. I suppose that was her second phone call to me in about five years.

When I was sixteen, one morning while riding to school through the streets of Bogotá, Colombia, a Jeep made a right turn into my bicycle. (This is the same experience I mentioned in Chapter 3.) While I was sailing through the air to an unpleasant encounter with the asphalt and the remarkable sight of the Jeep's rear tire rolling over my leg, the entire experience was unfolding as a memory. I had already experienced the accident while dreaming. One might ask why I only remembered the dream when it was too late. To me, it is more interesting that I was honored with a little lesson in the nature of reality. Besides, my leg had interesting tire tracks, was not broken, and I had a fine excuse for doing poorly on my French exam.

On leaving a local Greek restaurant a few weeks ago, gyros-with-everything in hand, a clear sense or image of a man I almost never see and do not know well—save by his colorful local reputation—popped into my mind. He is a retired professor—about eighty—and an artist. A few minutes later, there was the gentleman in question, standing behind my car as I unlocked it. We exchanged pleasantries. He suggested I back up over him, his tone playful, his eyes glinting with something not quite so playful. I declined with a lame comment of some sort and saw into the despair of growing old in a social world where age is an affliction and a disease.

Time bending, according to my informal surveys, is not all that rare. It is also, in my experience, not really very dramatic. It just happens, like knowing who is on the phone when it rings or what someone else is thinking. You will begin to become aware that you are time bending or "reading" other people's thoughts, however, through inner presence, especially through paying attention to the thoughts that "pop into your head." The importance of such phenomena are not necessarily in their utility but in their message. You may not always be right about who is on the phone before you pick it up, especially when you "try" to "know." When it does occur, time bending—the whole variety of nonverbal, transtemporal communications—remind us, explicitly and clearly, that our mind consciousness is not confined in space-time. Realizing that is boundary work. It is a tentative step out of Level II.

SYNCHRONICITIES: DISCOVERING THE WEB

Carl Jung, with the interested contributions of physicist Wolfgang Pauli, proposed the concept of synchronicity as an "acausal connecting principle." Jung was in search of a model, a precept, that would help him account for the designs he had seen again and again, in his own life and in many years of clinical practice.[2]

Becoming aware of the synchronicities in your life is valuable in personal transformation because they allow you direct experience of the web of nonlocal connection in which all of us dwell. More important, after you become used to living *in* the synchronicities of your life, the patterns of nonaccidental arrangement that unfold around you every day will become steadily more apparent. As that happens, your ability to sense the sacred flares of meaning behind ordinary appearance becomes better developed.

I have been familiar with little synchronicities for years. Often, since I've devoted a lot of time to being a writer and a college teacher, I've reached for just the right book and opened it to the right place. I honestly think my doctoral dissertation would have taken far longer without this fairly steady stream of synchronous "discoveries."

More recently, the patterns of nonlocal connection in my life have been more apparent to me. I seem almost continuously to be "coincidentally" running across people at "coincidental" times, for example.

Among the most puzzling synchronicities I've experienced over the last few years—for many synchronicities are puzzling—has been my intersection with a set of numerals: 11:11. I first became aware of that pattern on digital clock displays. I would notice 11:11 as I passed a bank. Later, 11:11 "signals" from clocks or other sources began to seem like a homing beacon. One could say that I simply became sensitized to that particular symmetry of numerals and began to look for it. Perhaps. But when I've consciously sought out that configuration, on a digital-clock display, for example, I do not experience it in the same way. More often, when I do get an 11:11 "signal," it will be at a very particular moment, at a moment that is clearly meaningful for me. When contemplating the painful fact that my marriage was no longer viable, facing the heart- and gut-wrenching business of finding a place to live, I ordered my new telephone number. The sum of the first two and last two digits of the four-digit number assigned me is 11 and 11. (Go ahead. Make your day. Pick up the phone book and see how many of the four-digit numbers meet that criterion.) On asking for a printout of checks at the credit union on December 21, 1994, the day of the winter solstice, my checking-account balance was, precisely, $1,111.94.

I should mention, by the way, that I've learned that the peculiar configuration of numerals, 11:11, has seemed to be a "homing beacon" of some sort to lots of people besides me. I came across a group of "11:11" people in Charlottesville, Virginia, who have developed a mythos and a metaphysical cosmology around it. Some of my New Age friends inform me that 11:11 is a consciousness-transformation signal, a sort of general wake-up call currently resonating through our collective consciousness. Maybe it is. Whatever it is, out of simply paying attention, I know it has something to do with my life. It probably has something to do with this book. Matrix theory is about a fourfold structure of what is, finally, one—our mind consciousness.

In any case, the general effect of becoming aware of the web of synchronicities, of discovering a pattern as your life unfolds, is a bit humbling. You may begin to recognize that your carefully laid plans and sensible assumptions are partial and limited. You may also begin to sense, then to know, that there are forces guiding your life that are transcendent of your conscious (Level II) intentions.

If you are not already doing so, you might try watching for patterns of coincidence—without judgment—using objective and inner presence. When "impossible coincidences" happen, honor them. In moments of intimacy, share what you are experiencing if you feel you can. To discover the web is to honor who you are; to share what you are learning is a way of touching the illuminated boundary of the self beyond the ego.

Try to let your awareness of meaningful "coincidences" be effortless. The power of the natural self is spontaneous, graceful, and simple. In this regard, mystical traditions offer a strange and compelling insight into enlightenment. To find the self, you need only fall into the natural flow of what is already there, already present in you. Think "effortless effort." Remember the lesson of sages and mystics: "I need do nothing."

FORMING LINKS BETWEEN CONSCIOUSNESS LEVELS

The quest for the self beyond the ego is, explicitly, inner work. It is about changing the way your mind consciousness is typically focused. But what that may involve for you will certainly have to do with your present life situation. For most of us socialized into Western culture, long periods devoted to silence and contemplation are very difficult. Our lives are full of alarm clocks and schedules. Many of us feel drained by just getting to work, preparing meals, and meeting the endless demands of raising our

children. Even setting aside a few minutes for silence and meditation may seem terribly difficult. In fact, my impression is that
people often have to change their entire lifestyles to pursue spiritual paths. Those who are able to manage that may be offering
all of us an important service as they explore new ways of living.
But many of us do not feel we can manage a move to our own
version of Walden Pond. I believe it was Krishnamurti who said
once that if you would seriously pursue a spiritual path, you must
learn to make your living with your left foot. For those of us who
need both our feet, there are simpler ways.

Guided by the logic of the Brenden Matrix, my sense of how
to proceed with inner work is, simply, one of finding a balance.
Your objective, after all, through self-honesty and desire tracking, is replacing ineffective and unconscious core-need strategies
with effective, conscious ones.

To that end, even as you read these words, you can decide to enter
into the "walking meditation" of just living, moment by moment.
Moment by moment, you may use objective and inner presence to
open windows in your awareness, to allow fragrant and exotic
breezes to blow into your life from beyond the consensus trance.

Reality Games

Exploring the patterns of our intentionality while in search of the
grounding of intent, of conscious choosing, is our central challenge. Do not misunderstand this, though. The New Age dictum
"You create your own reality" is almost meaningless in Level II
consciousness. At that level it can only mean that if you work hard
and follow the rules of the social world, you will be rewarded. And
that is often anything but the case. I believe we do, indeed, create
or manifest the conditions of our lives out of some level of awareness, but it may not be the one we are in touch with. Just as the
capabilities of your body are a function of your consciousness
state, the relationship between your consciousness level and your

control over manifestation is a function of your ability to exercise clear, conscious intent. We most certainly *can* begin to learn how intent is related to what happens around us and in our lives. We may also trust that at higher levels of consciousness, when what we want is in alignment with who we are, conscious manifestation happens. It is probably more or less automatic. For, however it works, it is quite probably the manner in which anything manifests in the universe. Reflecting on the demise of the classical Newtonian world view in the light of relativity and quantum physics, Sir James Jeans mused that the universe was turning out to be more like a great thought than a great machine. Here we will be more concise: All manifestation is mind stuff.

In my kitchen is a Dale Earnhardt racing car. It's a bank; I put quarters in it. I'm not really a stock-car racing fan, but I saved the model-car bank as a reminder. About two years ago, at a Christmas party for schoolteachers—one of whom I was married to at the time—a number of party-prize items were laid out on a table. They were mostly rather silly items donated by local businesses. We all drew numbers that might win us one of these prizes. Deciding I didn't want a John Deere cap or anything much else on the table, I "decided" I would have the racing-car bank. I'd give it to one of my boys, I thought.

The evening unfolded, numbers were read, someone else got the John Deere cap, and I waited, "knowing" I was going to get the racing car. I did. It is difficult to explain nonlinear, relational experiences in linear language. But the racing car was already mine; I'd imaged it. I had formed a clear intent. The intent unfolded. I wasn't even surprised. But I did honor the incident and the little metal car. Since my boys are more into Nintendo games than racing cars, they didn't really want it, so I kept it as a reminder. We begin to consciously manifest our life experiences when we begin to express intent in place of intentionality. To sort out the difference between these two things has concerned us in various ways throughout these pages. Now we will consider the difference in practical terms.

Intent and Intentionality

The world we see around us emerges out of a nonspatial, nontemporal matrix of potential, a relational order. Physicist and philosopher David Bohm called this web of relationships the "implicate order." When we act in the world, we draw this potential, this range of probabilities, into the realm of appearances and objectivities. When we do this consciously, we are exercising intent. When we do it unconsciously, we express patterns of intentionality.

Figure 2: Relationships of Intent and Intentionality to Manifestation

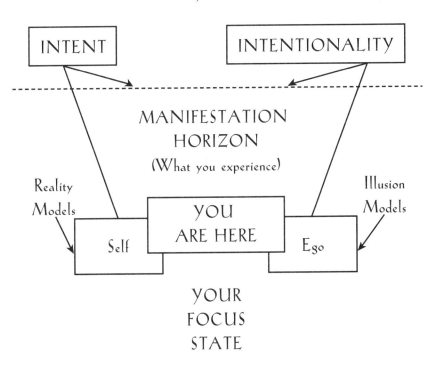

THE RELATIONAL ORDER
Which includes a . . .
PROBABILITY CONTINUUM

INTENT

INTENTIONALITY

MANIFESTATION
HORIZON
(What you experience)

Reality
Models

Illusion
Models

Self

YOU
ARE HERE

Ego

YOUR
FOCUS
STATE

We form intent or intentionality out of desire. Our desire nature, when out of alignment, manifests an illusion model, expressed as intentionality (an unconscious life path). Our body state, thoughts, and actions produce and reinforce an illusion model. And that's what you experience. As you allow self-knowledge to form a reality model, your desire nature can express itself as intent and you begin to manifest what you desire. You may learn who you are by learning what you want. You may manifest what you want by intent appropriate to who you are.

TRYING TO STAY AT LEVEL III

Out of the wisdom of the Brenden Matrix, there are four principles of life action. Recognizing them may help us remember where we are going in the journey out of ego entrancement. Here is a final matrix set.

FIGURE 3: FOUR PRINCIPLES OF ACTION

Two Modes of Knowing

	Relational	Objective
Self	Love	Empowerment
Not-Self	Commitment	Trust

COMMITMENT

It is an appropriate and authentic part of the quest for the self that you should ask why you are here. It is also appropriate that you should trust in and expect to discover your answer. Discovering your life task is part of entering into the Flow, part of leaving Level II. But, for most of us, the answer to this ultimate "cosmic question" will unfold, probably as we are ready for it.

While waiting for knowing to replace intermittent hunches, there are clues. Joseph Campbell's "Follow your bliss" motto is one of them. What gives you a sense of joy and of meaning is probably related to your life plan, since you are what you want, after all. You can also be pretty certain that whatever roles you are playing in your social world are wrong for you if they will not allow you to unfold, to enact, your cosmic-grounding need strategies. When you can manage it, your work and your play should allow you to be a channel for transcendent love (agape) expressed as empowering filial love as you play your social games.

While it is probably wise to understand that the life circumstances you are in are precisely the circumstances you need, it is probably not a good idea to assume that your life drama, as you ordinarily conceive it, is the way to salvation. While we live with egos at Level II, our life games are rather like dreams. They have no ontological substance in and of themselves. Career plans are not paths of salvation, in spite of Max Weber's insight into the way the "Protestant work ethic" developed in Western culture. Any social game, like your body, is either a useful vehicle for channeling life energy or it is not. Whether you fulfill your life task as a day-care worker, a taxi driver, or an attorney is probably not very important. Your part in the web of transformation may well call on powers you do not even imagine in yourself at present, but your work, pursued as you pay attention and surrender ego judgment, may be guided out of a level of knowing that is beyond ordinary thinking and planning.

In Level III consciousness, choosing is alignment and intent is spontaneous, guided by intuition and patterns of synchronicity. If you are a Christian, you may call this inner source the Holy Spirit. Ralph Waldo Emerson called it the "oversoul."[3] Taoists might call it "the Way." The Lakota shaman called it "walking in a sacred manner." But it does not matter what you call it. It is you in touch with your Source, acting as a channel for love's healing and transformative power.

While you are in search of your life task, commitment has two dimensions—assurance that you have such a task and patience as you move toward knowing what it is.

LOVE

The forms of love—agape, eros, filia, and storge—are the fulfillment of our core needs. As we saw in Chapter 8, when we are not acting in love, we are not pursuing effective core-need strategies.

EMPOWERMENT

When we feel that we cannot empower ourselves without taking power from another, we are pursuing ineffective, and probably unconscious, core-need strategies. In the web of connection that enfolds all of our lives, empowerment is a joint enterprise. To add power to the web, to empower and honor yourself, honor and empower every person who comes into your life. Everyone you know comes bearing gifts; everyone you meet needs your gifts. The wrapping paper for all of these gifts is awareness. Pay attention.

TRUST

Learning that your plans are not as important as your insights and your intuitions, that manifestation does not follow planning but intent, requires trust. While nothing is more challenging in the quest for the self, the practice of radical trust is truly exhilarating.

Trust that your body tends to heals itself, that healing is natural.

Trust that your mind moves always toward wholeness.

Trust that your four core needs are fulfilled by the forms of love.

Trust that abundance is all around you. You will have what you need when you need it.

Love, empowerment, trust, and commitment are anchoring principles of personal transformation, a fourfold way to balance and to self-knowledge.

BRENDEN'S FIRE

And now, having done some work at balancing head and heart, using the analytical and objective forms of Brenden's Matrix-for-choosing, let us transform what we may take from this learning into a single symbol, no longer objective, but relational. We do this to recall that our joint task, however we conceive it, whatever our part in the Design, must be to see through the ancient veil between the relational and the objective, the feminine and the masculine, the fire and the rose, the whole and the part. If we do not take up this task, our time on Earth will close and the story of humankind will end.

But that is not what we would choose; it is not what we are choosing. We are still the magical children who came here to learn what we might be. This sacred Earth, this crucible of transformation, is our heritage, and we will not choose death over life or fear over love.

In the symbol that ends this book, we can remember all that Brenden's Matrix may teach us and a little more, perhaps. For this symbol, without words, is a token of work become play, of time become timeless, of ingenuity in life's service, of harmony restored, of beauty honored, of fear's shadows burned away by light. It is what remains when illusion and dis-illusion are transmuted by the passion of the quest for the self, by Brenden's fire. Out of that alchemy, now worldless, a different thing must at last appear.

I offer you a sign of that transformation. The form of this sign, the Circle of Brighid, is a blending of heart and head from the heart and skill of an artist, Elizabeth Foster, who lent her insight into the personal and spiritual meaning of the Brenden Matrix. It is offered here in the spirit of gratitude by which we may receive the symbols of so many peoples and traditions across the panorama of our shared human adventure. Among the rich and wonderful forms out of American cultures, out of Africa, from Melanesia and Australia, out of the mists of Minoan Crete, from Hinduism, Buddhism, and Taoism, from medieval monasteries and aging cathedrals, this is one star from a million million stars. Its form emerges from the Celtic ancestry and traditions shared by both the artist and the writer.

It is a love token.

NOTES

Honoring simplicity as virtue, I have kept the notes in the body of the text to a minimum, some sources being given in context.

CHAPTER ONE: A DOOR OPENING

1. Important writings about planetary change include the visionary, analytical works of writers like Fritjof Capra, *The Turning Point* (New York: Bantam Books, 1982); Willis W. Harman, *Global Mind Change* (Indianapolis: Knowledge Systems, 1988); and Marilyn Ferguson, *The Aquarian Conspiracy* (Los Angeles: J. P. Tarcher, 1980), among many others. As a matter of fact, though, my ideas about change in the current era begin with the much earlier writings of sociologist and social philosopher P. A. Sorokin. (See chapter 2, note 12, below.)

In my view, the unprecedented planetwide change currently enveloping our species may be seen as an interactive convergence of three forces: (1) ecological change driven by human population growth; (2) social turbulence (linked in large measure to accumulating social and psychological effects of our commodity-for-profit-driven mode of production); and (3) shifts in perspective about the nature of reality, driven by the sciences. Among excellent works on planetary change, one in my view is unique for grasping an ecological perspective on our island Earth. That is James Lovelock, *The Ages of Gaia* (New York: W. W. Norton, 1988).

While this work addresses the second point in one way, as do the works of Capra, Ferguson, and Harman in another, important perspective on what Capra calls our "crisis of perception" are offered by Hazel Henderson in works like *Paradigms in Progress: Life Beyond Economics* (Indianapolis: Knowledge Systems, 1991) and, with respect to relations between men and women, Riane Eisler, *The Chalice and the Blade* (San Francisco: Harper & Row, 1987).

Among works that will introduce crucial changes in the sciences, I recommend Fritjof Capra, *The Tao of Physics* (New York: Bantam, 1983); Robert M. Augros and George N. Stanciu, *The New Story of Science* (New York: Bantam, 1984); Gary Zukav, *The Dancing Wu Li Masters* (New York: Bantam, 1979); and John Briggs and David Peat, *Turbulent Mirror: An Illustrated Guide to Chaos Theory and the Science of Wholeness* (New York: Harper & Row, 1989).

2. Michael Polanyi, *The Tacit Dimension* (New York: Doubleday Anchor Books, 1967).

CHAPTER TWO: BASIC IDEAS FROM MATRIX THEORY

1. Frank Waters, *Book of the Hopi* (New York: Ballantine, 1963), p. 33. Beyond Waters's book, I have drawn some insight into Hopi culture from the famous ethnography of a related culture, the Zuni, in Ruth Benedict, *Patterns of Culture* (New York: Houghton Mifflin, 1934), and from a remarkably fine ethnographic documentary, *Hopi: Songs of the Fourth World*, produced by the University of Arizona.

2. Zev ben Shimon Halevi, *Kabbalah: Tradition of Hidden Knowledge* (London: Thames and Hudson, 1979), edited by Warren Kenton.

3. Joseph Campbell, *Primitive Mythology: The Masks of God* (Penguin Books, 1987). Another interesting support for fourfold classifications in preliterate societies is Emile Durkheim and Marcel Mauss, *Primitive Classification* (Chicago: University of Chicago Press, 1963), trans. by Rodney Needham.

4. E. F. Schumacher, *A Guide for the Perplexed* (New York: Harper & Row, 1977).

5. William Irwin Thompson, *At the Edge of History* (New York: Harper & Row, 1971). Thompson's insights into William Butler Yeats, *A Vision* (New York: Collier Books, 1938), led me to explore that work. Yeats's rather mysterious and challenging treatment of consciousness and personality was channeled through his wife, making it an inherently controversial source of support for my notion that the Brenden Matrix represents what I call an ontomorph or "being-form." Thompson himself develops a fourfold model out of Yeats in chapter 4 of *Edge*, which was my first exciting encounter with a body of ideas that made me see that my fourfold invention—developed first out of an analysis of Max Weber's theory of action (about ten years before encountering Thompson)—was not hopelessly odd. Although I construct my Brenden Matrix differently from Thompson, the feel of his explorations evoked in me a clear sense that we were probing the same mysterious geography. Further, his insights into fundamental role types provided a "launch point," which would help me find sociological uses for the Brenden Matrix.

6. Alan Page Fiske, *Structures of Social Life: The Four Elementary Forms of Human Relations* (New York: The Free Press, 1991). Fiske acknowledges a debt to Talcott Parsons, including Parsons and Bales's theory of action. Therein, the four-function paradigm—Integration, Goal Attainment, Adaptation, and the Latency Function—are proposed as an analytical approach to social-system homeostasis. For an updated summary treatment,

see Peter Knapp, *One World, Many Worlds: Contemporary Sociological Theory* (New York: HarperCollins, 1994), chapter 7.

7. Joseph Campbell, ed., *The Portable Jung*, trans. by R. F. C. Hull (New York: Viking Press, 1971), includes Jung's basic writings on the psychic functions and on personality types.

8. Carl G. Jung, *Lectures in Analytical Psychology* (New York: Vintage Books, 1968), p. 62.

9. In particular, as Peter Farb explains, Korzybski isolated a logical contradiction of language: it is meant to convey experience, yet by its very nature it is incapable of doing so. See Farb's *Word Play* (New York: Bantam, 1973), pp. 193–94.

10. William James, *Psychology: The Briefer Course* (New York: Harper & Row, 1961), ed. by Gordon Allport. James, in fact, makes what I call a primary existential division between "me" and "not-me." In proposing different sorts of "mes"—material, social, and spiritual (p. 58 and following)—James is not far from proposing the facets of the self we offer here as a matrix set.

11. Robert Ornstein, *The Psychology of Consciousness* (San Francisco: W. H. Freeman & Co., 1972), p. 67.

12. The table gathers together a number of sources. Below, sources associated with individual thinkers are given in order of the last name of the author.

David Bohm, *Wholeness and the Implicate Order* (London: Ark, 1980). Bohm, author of a classical text in quantum mechanics, deals with a range of concerns in this seminal work, some of them relating our ideas about consciousness to a unified field approach to semantic structure and thought. His essential insight is *wholeness*. To quote him: ". . . wholeness is what is real . . . fragmentation is the response of this whole to man's action guided by illusory perception, which is shaped by fragmentary thought" (p. 7). His fairly famous metaphor for the implicate order—a droplet of ink stirred into a container of clear glycerin—is given on p. 149.

Martin Buber, *I and Thou*, 2d ed. (New York: Charles Scribner's Sons, 1958).

Emile Durkheim, *The Division of Labor in Society* (New York: The Free Press, 1964), is the famous doctoral dissertation in which Durkheim elaborates his distinction between mechanical and organic solidarity.

Dorothy Lee, "Codifications of Reality: Lineal and Nonlineal," *Psychosomatic Medicine* 12, no. 2 (1950): 89–97.

Michael Polanyi, *The Tacit Dimension* (New York: Doubleday Anchor, 1967).

P. A. Sorokin, *Social and Cultural Dynamics*, 4 vols. (New York: Bedminster Press, 1938–41). Sorokin's hypothesis of oscillating cultural mentalities, from ideational (relational) to sensate (objective), is documented with awe-inspiring analyses of many aspects of Western culture, such as law, philosophy, and even patterns of war. His analysis of art as an indicator of cultural mentality, for example, catalogs and analyzes virtually every major museum piece available in the United States and Europe from about 500 B.C. on.

Ferdinand Toennies, *Community and Society* (New York: Harper & Row, 1957). The translation of Toennies's major work (*Gemeinschaft und Gesellschaft*) outlines the distinctive cultural mentalities I would identify as relational (*Gemeinschaft*—person-centered society) and objective (*Gesellschaft*—corporate society).

13. William James, *Essays in Radical Empiricism* (New York: 1912), ed. by R. B. Perry.

14. Allport's "saliva example" of the arbitrary boundary between the self and the not-self is cited by James W. Vander Zanden, *Social Psychology* (New York: Random House, 1987), p. 146.

15. The idea of the body as a field of energy information is discussed in a delightful way by Deepak Chopra on an audiotape production, *The Higher Self*, 6 audio cassettes (Nightingale Conant, 1992).

16. Listen to Chopra, *ibid.*, for an intuitively engaging and nontechnical way of thinking about the idea that "matter is mind stuff."

17. Arthur Koestler, *The Roots of Coincidence* (New York: Vintage Books, 1972). In this exploration of synchronicity and "paranormal" phenomena, Koestler introduces his concept of systems as "Janus-faced holons."

18. Philosopher Alfred North Whitehead, through his notion of prehensive unification, lends us interesting insights into the relationship of what is "outside" of us as perceptual objects are constructed in our actual experience. See, for example, Whitehead's *Science and the Modern World* (New York: The Free Press, 1957, original copyright 1925). In a unified-field approach to reality, one in which mind and matter are not separable, the very least one may say is that a rose exists as a *product* of mind and of our perception of the rose. These issues are clarified and updated by Gregory Bateson in *Mind and Nature: a Necessary Unity* (New York: Bantam, 1979).

19. Fiske, *Structures of Social Life* (New York: The Free Press, 1991).

20. Talcott Parsons, *Societies* (Englewood Cliffs, N.J.: Prentice Hall, 1966).

21. A brief treatment of James's thought, which conveys some of the sense of what is meant by radical empiricism, is found in Morton White, ed., *The Age of Analysis* (New York: New American Library, 1955).

CHAPTER THREE: WHAT TO DO WITH A BRENDEN MATRIX

1. Deepak Chopra, *Unconditional Life: Mastering the Forces That Shape Personal Reality* (New York: Bantam Books, 1991).

2. A pioneer in tracking down the common essence of the great religious traditions was Aldous Huxley, in *The Perennial Philosophy* (New York: Harper & Brothers, 1945). He notes that harmlessness is a common theme in the world's great mystical traditions—although that principle has often been aborted in cultures informed by "religions of the Book," Christianity, Islam, and Judaism. Another approach to the essence underlying worldwide mystical teachings is found in Huston Smith, *Forgotten Truth: The Primordial Tradition* (New York: Harper & Row, 1976).

CHAPTER FOUR: CHOOSING

1. The linking of social consciousness to the mode of production is a common theme in many sociological works, from Marx to modern structural-functionalists like Talcott Parsons. I suppose the classic quick introduction to this sort of linkage is Marx and Engels, *The Communist Manifesto,* but more conservative structural ideas with the same rough purport come out of the Durkheimian tradition (see citations under note 12 in chapter 2) as well as from Gerhard Lenski in works like *Human Societies,* 4th ed. (New York: McGraw Hill, 1980). Anthropologist Peter Farb illustrates relationships of culture to the mode of production in *Man's Rise to Civilization as Shown by the Indians of North America* (New York: E. P. Dutton, 1968).

2. Insight into the emphasis on relational-mode knowing in preliterate tribal cultures is available from a number of sources. One of the more accessible and interesting may be John Neihardt, *Black Elk Speaks* (Lincoln: University of Nebraska Press, 1979). Neihardt's classic is an interpretive narrative taken from a dialogue with a Holy Man of the Oglala Sioux (Lakota). A more recent, if controversial, insight into Australian aboriginal culture comes from an account by Marlo Morgan of her courageous journey through the outback with a "wild" band in *Mutant Message Down Under* (New York: HarperCollins, 1994.)

3. Pitirim A. Sorokin, a neglected voice in American sociology, proposed the alternation of cultural mentalities in the West from ideational to sensate. His main work in support of this thesis is the monumental *Social and Cultural Dynamics* (New York: Bedminster Press, 1938–1941). Sorokin's ideas have been put into the context of models of current global change by both Hazel Henderson in, for example, *The Politics of the Solar Age: Alternatives to*

Economics (Indianapolis: Knowledge Systems, 1988), and Fritjof Capra, *The Turning Point* (New York: Bantam Books, 1982).

4. Max Weber, *The Protestant Ethic and the Spirit of Capitalism* (New York: Charles Scribner's Sons, 1958). His "iron cage" metaphor appears at the closing of the last chapter.

5. Joseph Chilton Pearce, *Magical Child: Rediscovering Nature's Plan for Our Children* (New York: Bantam, 1977). Pearce continues and elaborates on the war of culture against our human potential in an important work, *Evolution's End: Claiming the Potential of Our Intelligence* (HarperSanFrancisco, 1992). One could, perhaps, consider parallel approaches between Pearce's neurophysiological insights and the intuitive, experientially oriented, notions of matrix theory.

6. See Kenneth Ring, *Heading Toward Omega* (New York: William Morrow, 1985), for an excellent summary of the data on NDEs and their implications. A remarkable and profound book on near-death experiences is P. M. H. Atwater, *Coming Back to Life: The After-Effects of the Near-Death Experience* (New York: Dodd, 1988). Atwater is, herself, a near-death experiencer.

7. Gary Zukav, *The Seat of the Soul* (New York: Simon & Schuster, 1989).

CHAPTER FIVE: BRENDEN MATRIX GEOMETRY: THE QUEST FOR WHAT WE REALLY WANT

1. Eric Hoffer, *The True Believer* (New York: Harper & Brothers, 1951).

2. Ingo Swann, *To Kiss Earth Goodbye* (New York: Dell Publishing, 1975.)

CHAPTER SIX: OUR CORE-NEED GEOMETRY: STILL LOOKING FOR WHAT WE REALLY WANT

1. James Redfield, in *The Celestine Prophecy* (New York: Warner Books, 1993), draws on the work of maverick existential psychologist Ronald Laing in proposing that people steal life energy from each other. In *The Politics of Experience* (New York: Ballantine Books, 1967), among other works, Laing is iconoclastic, to say the least, about conventional "loving" familial relationships. A single quote from *Politics* . . . should illustrate his point of view on what I call scarcity egonomics. "The family's function is to repress Eros; to induce a false consciousness of security; to deny death by avoiding life; to cut off transcendence; to believe in God, not to experience the void; to create, in short, one-dimensional man; to promote respect, conformity, obedience; to con children out of play; to induce a fear of failure" (p. 65).

CHAPTER SEVEN: OF MASKS AND FACES: LIFE IN THE CONSENSUS TRANCE

1. For an example of materialist reductionism by a popular science writer, see Jon Franklin, *Molecules of the Mind* (New York: Dell Publishing, 1987).

2. Rejections of materialist reductionism respecting the nature of mind come to us in powerful waves of insight from brain researcher Karl Pribram, who, influenced by physicist David Bohm, developed the holographic paradigm. See, for example, Michael Talbot, *The Holographic Universe* (New York: HarperCollins, 1991.) Another profound thinker opposing the "matter myth" is Roger Penrose in *The Emperor's New Mind* (New York: Oxford University Press, 1988). For a less technical rebuttal of what Robert M. Augros and George N. Stanciu call "the old story of science," see their book, *The New Story of Science* (New York: Bantam, 1984).

3. Sigmund Freud, *The Future of an Illusion,* trans. by James Strachey (New York: W. W. Norton, 1961).

CHAPTER EIGHT: CHOOSING II: THE POWER MATRIX

1. C. S. Lewis, *The Four Loves* (New York: Harcourt Brace Jovanovich, 1960).

2. *A Course in Miracles,* 3 vols. (Tiberon, Calif.: Foundation for Inner Peace, 1977), introduction to the text.

3. Raynor C. Johnson, *The Imprisoned Splendour* (Wheaton, Ill.: The Theosophical Publishing House, 1953), p. 309.

4. Joseph Chilton Pearce, *Exploring the Crack in the Cosmic Egg* (New York: Bantam, 1974), p. 123.

CHAPTER NINE: DOS* FOR DUMMIES

1. Robert A. Monroe, *Far Journeys* (New York: Doubleday, 1985).

2. What I call Level IV sources vary in clarity and what I think of as "transmission static"—the ego interference of the person "translating" the inner source material. I have been impressed and influenced by *A Course in Miracles* (Tiberon, Calif.: Foundation for Inner Peace, 1977). I have also found many useful ideas and insights in the "Seth" books of trance medium and poet Jane Roberts. These include *Seth Speaks: The Eternal Validity of the Soul* (Englewood Cliffs, N.J.: Prentice Hall, 1975) and *The Nature of Personal Reality* (Englewood Cliffs, N.J.: Prentice Hall, 1974). I also find much to value in Ken Carey, *Starseed: The Third Millennium* (HarperSanFrancisco, 1991); Gary Zukav, *The Seat of the Soul* (New York: Simon & Schuster, 1989); and Stewart Edward White, *The Unobstructed Universe* (New York: Dell Publishing, 1968), among many others.

CHAPTER TEN: IMMORTALITY

1. P. M. H. Atwater, *Coming Back to Life* (New York: Dodd, 1988).

2. Raymond Moody, M.D., *Reunions: Visionary Encounters with Departed Loved Ones* (New York: Ballantine Books, 1993).

3. Robert A. Monroe, *Far Journeys* (New York: Doubleday, 1985).

4. See the Level IV sources cited in note 2, chapter 9.

5. Kenneth Ring, *Heading Toward Omega* (New York: William Morrow, 1985).

6. Atwater, *Coming Back to Life.*

7. Ring, *Heading Toward Omega,* p. 34 and following.

8. Larry Dossey, M.D., *Recovering the Soul* (New York: Bantam, 1989), beginning on page 45. The actual study by Randolph Byrd is reported in "Positive Therapeutic Effects of Intercessory Prayer in a Coronary Care Unit Population," *Southern Medical Journal* 81, no. 7 (July 1988): 826–29.

9. The quote "Seek the Truth, come whence it may, come how it might," is inscribed on the library wall at Virginia Theological Seminary in Alexandria, Virginia. It made a deep impression on me.

CHAPTER ELEVEN: SILENT DAWN

1. See the comments on the nature of dreaming in Raynor C. Johnson, *The Imprisoned Splendour* (Wheaton, Ill.: The Theosophical Publishing House, 1953), p. 211.

2. Carl G. Jung, *Synchronicity: An Acausal Connecting Principle,* trans. by R. F. C. Hull (Princeton: Princeton University Press, 1969).

3. Ralph Waldo Emerson, "Self-Reliance" (1841), in *The Best of Ralph Waldo Emerson* (Roslyn, N.Y.: Walter J. Black, 1969), pp. 119–46.

GLOSSARY

Body Image In the ego, the projected or imagined idea of what one's body looks like to others.

Brenden Matrix The fourfold matrix formed by joining two pairs of paradoxically opposed yet complementary attitudes of human consciousness. One of these pairs is made up of the two ways of knowing: relational knowing, which is direct, nonverbal, and intuitive, and objective knowing, which is verbal, indirect, and linear-rational. The second paradoxical duality, called the primary existential division, reminds us that we divide all our experiences into domains we associate with "me" or the self, and an opposed domain we associate with "not-me" or the not-self. The construction of the matrix is explained in chapter 2.

Complementarity (1) A principle proposed by physicist Niels Bohr to explain paradoxes like the Heisenberg uncertainty principle (if you get a good measurement on where an electron is, you can't measure its momentum with accuracy, and vice versa). (2) In matrix theory, the simple observation that for every appearance of duality a third frame of reference is available that reconciles their opposition. Male and female are complementary states of body expression in humans reconciled by the common ground of the psyche, which is both male and female and can express either mode or form.

Consciousness At once the most obvious and the most mysterious dimension of our experience. For convenience, while we become initiates of the mystery, we may assume these things about personal consciousness (sometimes referred to as mind consciousness): It is a "field" connecting us to everything, everywhere. The part of this field we are tuned in to may be called a "consciousness state." Dreaming, ordinary waking awareness, and a mescaline trip are different consciousness states. (Chapter 9 explains four levels, each of which has distinct consciousness states associated with it.) When we move between states, as between dreaming and ordinary waking awareness, we make a "quantum jump" from one state to the other. All possible consciousness states are "running" (are aspects of your consciousness field, like electromagnetic bands at different frequencies), and you can, by changing your "receiver," tune in to any of them. We are doggedly inclined to remain tuned to low-frequency consciousness states. Apparently that is a cost of living in a body in time. What we may be *aware* of at any moment depends on our consciousness state. What is real (produces experiential effects) in one state may not be real in another state. The higher the consciousness level or state, the greater our freedom to select what we want to experience. It can be very confusing to be in a high-frequency state (as in a near-death experience), where you manifest what you want very rapidly, if you do not know what you want.

Consensus Trance A limited, shared world view promoted in a social world through conditioned perception, the limits of language, and the egolike defensiveness of societies.

Core Need The basic hypothesis of matrix theory is that human action and human social productions develop as humans attempt to meet four fundamental transcultural and transhistorical core needs. These are the need to give and receive love, the need for cosmic (spiritual) grounding, the need for identity and approval in a social world, and the need to nurture and protect the body.

Core-Need Strategy Any conscious or unconscious, effective or ineffective action aimed at satisfying a core need.

Cosmic Grounding The human core need associated with the psychic function we call "intuition." The cosmic-grounding core need is fulfilled in us through direct experience, which permits us to know that we are at home and safe in the universe.

Ego In matrix theory, the complex of conditioned attitudes and behavioral responses that develop through the process of socialization. The ego is a socially induced "security system" produced in us, inadvertently, by our parents and others close to us.

Eros The life energy that flows through every thought and action, even when that energy is negative or distorted. Eros is also one of four major forms of love, but its energy is expressed in all the other major forms—agape, storge, and filia—discussed in chapter 8.

Hierarchical Role Any social role that is ranked higher (or lower) than related roles—like nurse and doctor. Hierarchical roles are associated with our core need for social identity and approval.

Inception The way we know an inner world, including the self beyond the ego. In matrix theory, inception is seen as the complement of perception. Perception relates consciousness to what we encounter through the senses—

seeing, hearing, smelling, feeling, and tasting. Inception relates consciousness to what we perceive from within, including memory, feeling, and intuition. Inception is the primary channel for direct, relational knowing.

Instrumental Role Any social role we play that is associated with the core need for body nurturance and survival.

Legitimating Role Any social role we play that is directly or indirectly associated with our need for cosmic grounding. Examples include all those social roles that are expected to guide the thoughts and actions of others, such as teacher, physician, or mother. Hierarchical and legitimating roles are often linked together.

Mask The aspect of the ego we hold up to the world to gain the approval of ourselves and others. It contains our "ego ideal," an inner complex of ideas about how we should act in different social roles.

Matrix Set Any fourfold model that may reasonably be said to fit the general form of the Brenden Matrix. The four core needs, Carl Jung's four psychic functions, and Alan Fiske's four fundamental forms of social relations are examples of matrix sets described in chapter 2.

Matrix Theory The body of ideas derived from the theory of human core needs and the implications of the Brenden Matrix outlined in chapter 2. The theory proposes that humans have a "matrix" of four fundamental core needs, which motivate both our conscious and our unconscious behavior.

Natural Self Our potential "ground state" as human beings, mainly associated with our core need for giving and receiving love. In our natural or "child" self we are playful, curious, spontaneous, sensual, and sensitive to beauty.

Newton's Triangle Three attitudes or assumptions that typically underlie the way we think if we are raised in a Westernized culture. The three points of the triangle are materialism (the assumption that everything that is real is made of matter), objectivism (that matter things are separate and more or less unrelated), and determinism (which assumes that any phenomenon is an effect of matter affecting matter).

Not-Self We humans divide all our experience, all of the content of our consciousness, into two domains—self and not-self. The not-self domain includes everything we experience that appears not to be part of our self. Paradoxically, the two domains are not separable and, in fact, define each other as aspects of consciousness.

Nurturant Role Any social role through which we may, directly, express our core need for giving and receiving love.

Objective Knowing The complement of relational-mode knowing. Objective knowing is rational, linear, verbal-symbolic, indirect, and contingent on the limits of a particular cultural and historical period.

Ontomorph A "being form" (from the Greek *ontos*, being, and *morph*, form). The Brenden Matrix is a general form or model that represents a fourfold structure inherent in human mind consciousness. It represents an ontomorph.

Perception The way we know the outer, sensory world. Perception is selectively filtered through the ego.

Primary Existential Division We divide everything that enters conscious awareness into two categories, those we associate with the self and those we consider to be outside the self (not-self). The self/not-self division is one of the dualities that give rise to the Brenden Matrix.

Psychosocial Exclusion Principle When we are focused or "tuned in" to relational-mode knowing, the complementary mode, objective knowing, appears superficial and limited. When we are "tuned in" to the objective mode, relational-mode knowing appears dreamy, impractical, and mystical. Whole cultures tend to endorse one mode of knowing and to devalue its complement. Western culture is a "left-brained" or objective-mode culture. Preliterate cultures, like the Hopi, are "right-brained" or relational.

Relational Imperative A built-in but often hidden understanding that fruitful human action must follow the principles of harmlessness, nonjudgment, and forgiveness.

Relational Knowing Associated with our feeling and intuition, relational knowing, as the source of all knowing, is direct, nonverbal, and atemporal (not time-bound). Relational knowing is experienced directly as some form of "being-in-relationship."

Scarcity Egonomics Along with the generally hidden assumptions of Newton's triangle, the sort of awareness we have when we are operating out of our ego. The notion that death is the end of everything, that innocence is weakness, and that we are isolated and alone are among the principles of scarcity egonomics. (See chapter 7 for all of them.)

Self The term has two dimensions in this book. In constructing the Brenden Matrix, the self is the part of our experience we *may* identify with at any moment. The self is also who we really are, beyond the ego, whether we are aware of it or not.

Shadow In the ego, the aspect of consciousness that hides the natural self. The shadow may actually act like an "anti-ego," trying to teach us who we are in mischievous and surprising ways. Unlike other aspects of the ego, our shadow nature connects us to realms of consciousness beyond our awareness.

Socialization The process by which we learn language, social norms, and "self" norms in order to survive in a social world. It is the process by which we develop an ego, especially before about age four. After that, "secondary socialization" modifies the ego but seldom gives us ways to transcend it.

Superego Adapted from the Freudian concept, in matrix theory, the superego refers to all the ways we store guilt in our mind and body.

Transcendent Self The aspect of the self that connects us to the entire visible and invisible universe.

ABOUT THE AUTHOR

Robert Griffith Turner, Jr., was born at Schoffield Barracks, Oahu, Hawaii, in 1938. According to family lore, a notice posted in the maternity ward at Schoffield read: "No Children Allowed." He has been searching for his inner child ever since.

Robert has worked as a freelance writer, a print media designer, an artist-illuminator, and a regional magazine publisher. At present, he is an adjunct assistant professor of sociology at Virginia Tech and at Radford University. Beyond his efforts to understand the heart of human choosing and contribute to new ways of approaching the human sciences, he writes stage plays, novels, and essays. He lives in the mountains of Virginia, in Blacksburg, with a cat named Merlin.